Environmental Issues in Your Real Estate Practice

MARIE S. SPODEK, DREI, GRI
with BILL MAGARGAL

Second Edition

Dearborn™
Real Estate Education

This publication is designed to provide accurate and authoritative information in regard to the subject matter covered. It is sold with the understanding that the publisher is not engaged in rendering legal, accounting, or other professional service. If legal advice or other expert assistance is required, the services of a competent professional person should be sought.

President: Roy Lipner
Publisher: Evan Butterfield
Associate Publisher: Louise Benzer
Development Editor: Caitlin Ostrow
Managing Editor, Production: Daniel Frey
Typesetter: Janet Schroeder
Creative Director: Lucy Jenkins

Copyright 2004, 2005 by Dearborn™ Real Estate Education, a division of Dearborn Financial Publishing, Inc.®

Published by Dearborn™ Real Estate Education,
a division of Dearborn Financial Publishing, Inc.®
30 South Wacker Drive
Chicago, IL 60606-7481
(312) 836-4400
http://www.dearbornRE.com

All rights reserved. The text of this publication, or any part thereof, may not be reproduced in any manner whatsoever without permission in writing from the publisher.

Printed in the United States of America.

05 06 07   10 9 8 7 6 5 4 3 2 1

Library of Congress Cataloging-in-Publication Data

Spodek, Marie S.

Environmental issues in your real estate practice / Marie Spodek and Bill Magargal.-- 2nd ed.

   p. cm.

ISBN 0-7931-9261-7

1. Real estate agents--Training of--United States--Handbooks, manuals, etc.
2. Real property--Environmental aspects--United States.
3. Vendors and purchasers--United States. I. Magargal, Bill. II. Title.

HD278.S66 2005

333.33'068--dc22   2004025331

contents

About the Authors iv

part A — Practice and Liability Issues 1

Chapter 1 General Issues 3

part B — Indoor Environmental Issues 11

Chapter 2 Lead-Based Paint 13
Chapter 3 Radon 24
Chapter 4 Mold 34
Chapter 5 Asbestos 46
Chapter 6 Volatile Organic Compounds (VOCs) and Pesticides 54
Chapter 7 Drinking Water 65
Chapter 8 Other Indoor Issues 73

part C — Outdoor Environmental Pollutants 85

Chapter 9 Underground Storage Tanks (USTs) 87
Chapter 10 Waste Sites and Toxic Substances 93
Chapter 11 Construction Issues 101
Chapter 12 Wetlands, Watersheds, and Endangered Species 109
Chapter 13 Environmental Reports and Consultants 117

Appendix A: Major Environmental Laws 124
Answer Key 126
Glossary 140

about the authors

Marie S. Spodek, DREI, GRI, is a nationally recognized real estate educator, speaker, and trainer. A popular real estate columnist for several years and a former real estate licensee, she brings an informal, easy-to-read style and a wealth of practical experience to her professional publications. She is co-author of *Manufactured and Modular Housing*, consulting editor for *Property Management*, 7th edition, and a contributor to Dearborn's *Real Estate Basics* series.

In 1996, the U.S. Environmental Protection Agency recognized her for developing "Reducing Radon Risk in Real Estate Transactions," a course for real estate instructors. She is active in the National Association of REALTORS® and the Real Estate Educators Association (REEA), from which she received the Jack Wiedemer Distinguished Career Award in 2001.

Bill Magargal is a former research engineer, software developer, and IT director for a multinational corporation, with over 35 years of computer and design experience.

■ Acknowledgments

This edition was created with the help of valuable reviews by:

- Michael Buettner, Aerotech Laboratories Inc. and Aerotech Technical Institute
- Michael Fair, Illinois Academy of Real Estate
- Phyllis Lea Goodrich, Academy of Real Estate
- Margaret Nagel, Chicago Association of REALTORS® and REALTORS® Real Estate School

part A
Practice and Liability Issues

chapter one

General Issues

learning objectives

Upon completing this chapter, you will be able to

- list at least two environmental hazards of which a real estate licensee should be aware for each consumer: residential, commercial, or developers.
- explain why environmental concerns often surface during real estate transactions.
- discuss why clients expect assistance from their real estate agent.
- explain the value of seller property disclosure forms and what they do not cover.
- list five rules to follow that can keep an agent out of trouble.
- consult a list of sources for gaining additional information.

■ Key Terms

caveat emptor   disclosure forms   U S. Environmental
                                                         Protection Agency
                                                         (EPA)

■ What Is Different about Real Estate Transactions Today?

Today there is more to a real estate transaction than simply bringing together a buyer and seller. In the past, licensees controlled virtually all information pertinent to a real estate transaction. Today, buyers and sellers routinely use the Internet to find properties, evaluate neighborhoods, compare prices, and so on. The days of innocence are gone; the age of information is here.

Real estate professionals are now being seen as "gatekeepers" in transactions. As such, clients and customers of real estate professionals expect to be informed about environmental hazards. If environmental problems arise, buyers and sellers frequently turn to agents and brokers for information about service providers.

Why Have Environmental Issues Become a Big Concern?

For decades, the doctrine of *caveat emptor* (buyer beware) governed most real estate transactions, and real estate licensees generally represented only the seller. Any contingencies written into sales agreements were normally limited to structural concerns such as leaking, flooding, and pests.

However, things began to change in 1969 when Congress passed the National Environmental Policy Act. The act created and funded the Environmental Protection Agency (EPA), which raised the national awareness of various environmental issues. But it was not until 1978 that environmental laws began to impact real estate transfers at all, and that involved lead hazard removal in public housing. In 1992, Congress passed the Lead-Based Paint Hazardous Reduction Act (LBPHRA). This precedent-setting act was the first time that the federal government became involved in residential real estate transfer, and it introduced the concept of "disclosure" in real estate sales situations.

In the years since LBPHRA, other environmental concerns have become part of the real estate lexicon. Unlike lead-based paint, these have not been required by federal statute. Instead, they became real estate issues after large civil lawsuits resulted in huge judgments against brokers, agents, and sellers for failure to disclose various environmental problems. As a result, disclosure of numerous conditions is routine in most residential real estate transactions.

Although there is no good time to raise environmental issues, in many cases these issues can be dealt with easily and successfully early in the transaction. The key to a successful closing involves timely and reliable testing to determine if there is a hazard, and if so, to disclose, early and often.

However, few states mandate disclosures during transactions involving raw land and commercial or industrial properties. This does not mean that these sellers should not make disclosures, but they are not required to do so by statute. Licensees who work with these buyers are advised to raise environmental concerns with their clients.

Do All Consumers Have the Same Concerns?

Each category of the real estate industry concentrates on different environmental priorities. For instance, residential real estate agents must be aware of indoor air pollution, lead-based paint, and asbestos as well as proximity to industrial or commercial activities that produce pollutants. Commercial real estate agents and property managers are also concerned with asbestos, indoor air quality, and lead-based paint. However, if the property is undeveloped, then attention must be paid to wetlands, endangered species, toxic waste sites, water supply sources, and storage tanks (above or underground).

The residential buyer may never have had his own home tested for any hazard, but now wants his new one to be perfect: no termites, no radon, no lead paint, no leaks. Now, residential real estate agents find themselves increasingly asked about environmental issues.

■ What Do Consumers Want from Real Estate Licensees?

Clients and customers expect to be given not only information about environmental issues before they need it but also assistance in dealing with problems if and when they arise. This assistance may become especially important if state or federal laws do not address the issues.

Consumer protection is an important part of any real estate transaction, and today's buyers and sellers are educated, conscious of health and safety, and insistent about having detailed information to make informed, rational decisions. Their concern and care is warranted. Environmental damage may not always be apparent, and an owner's ignorance of the problem may not relieve an owner of liability. With full disclosure, buyers and sellers enter a level playing field on which they can negotiate equitable solutions.

Clients turn to the real estate professional for advice. While real estate licensees need not be specialists, they should be familiar with environmental hazards, problems, and concerns that are common in their marketplaces. Licensees must also be aware of the laws, rules, and regulations that are there to protect the consumer and the environment.

■ What about Property Disclosure Forms?

In the past, disclosure of latent material facts was generally required. However, today most states require sellers to make detailed property disclosures of numerous environmental issues as well.

In some jurisdictions, agents accept seller-supplied disclosure forms without question, believing that what they don't know can't hurt them. However, this posture is becoming increasingly risky.

Some states, particularly California, impose a burden on the agent to discover problems and to ask about red flags. This presumption that an agent should have known requires additional investigative work on the part of the real estate licensee. For instance, if a pipe is seen protruding from the ground, one should not assume that it is a submarine!

Equally important, licensees should caution buyers not to rely on disclosure forms as either a warranty or a guarantee. Rather, they are an assignment of responsibility. Sellers are required to honestly disclose issues of which they are aware. Buyers are put on notice that not only do they have the right but also the duty to discover hazards about which they are concerned. The seller states what he has or does not have, or knows or does not know. Absence of knowledge by the seller certainly does not mean the property is hazard-free.

Very early in the process, the licensee should determine the buyer's attitude regarding specific environmental hazards. For example, if testing discloses interior radon levels above some particular value, what reading levels will the client accept? Will the client accept mitigation, removal, or neither?

What Rules Should Agents Follow to Avoid Trouble?

Generally, licensees can avoid trouble by not making decisions for their clients. If there is a question of whether to disclose or not, then the seller should disclose. If a buyer expresses any concern, take it seriously. In addition, agents should remember the *BREAD* principles below:

- **Know the Basics:** Learn the basics of environmental hazards, how they can potentially harm people, and what can be done to prevent any such harm. Become familiar with what the law requires and how to handle frequently encountered situations.
- **Keep Records:** Licensees should routinely jot down all key activities and the dates they occurred as part of their standard business practices. Remember, if it's in writing you have a chance, if not . . . well, it depends on the circumstances.
- **Call the Experts:** In addition to knowing the basics, licensees should know who the experts are and how to contact them. Almost always, one should check with the U.S. Environmental Protection Agency (EPA), especially its excellent Web sites. Other sources of expertise in environmental issues include the state departments of natural resources, the local health department, or the American Lung Association.
- **Ask Questions:** How many questions to ask depends on the state. As previously noted, some states impose an additional duty on real estate brokers, i.e., a broker is responsible not only for what is known or accessible to him, but also for what he/she "should have known." On the opposite side of the fence are the states that operate under the philosophy of caveat emptor, or "let the buyer beware."
- **Disclose early and often:** Disclosure of information to both the buyer and seller early in the transaction is very helpful. Early education and discussion gives both parties time to decide what they want to do about environmental hazards and helps them make their own informed decisions.

Where Can I Get More Information?

The EPA is the best place to start. Its Web sites are excellent and comprehensive. The Web site address is *http://www.epa.gov*. Following are other organizations to contact for specific information that supplements what the EPA offers.

- **National Center for Environmental Publications and Information (NCEPI)**
  Box 42419
  Cincinnati, OH 45242
  (800) 490-9198
  http://www.epa.gov/ncepihom
  email: *ncepimal@one.net*
- **U.S. Consumer Protection Safety Commission (CPSC)**
  (800) 638-2772
  http://www.cpsc.gov/
- **Indoor Air Quality Information Clearinghouse (IAQ INFOR)**
  PO Box 37133
  Washington, DC 20013-7133
  (800) 438-4318

- **U.S. Environmental Protection Agency**
  Ariel Rios Building
  1200 Pennsylvania Avenue, N.W.
  Washington, DC 20460
  (202) 272-0167
  http://www.epa.gov
- **National Radon Hotline**
  (800) SOS-RADON
- **National Lead Information Center**
  (800) 424-LEAD (5323)
  http://www.epa.gov/lead/nlic.htm
- **National Pesticides Information Center**
  (800) 858-PEST (7378)
  http://npic.orst.edu/
  email: *npic@ace.orst.edu*
- **RCRA/Superfund Hotline**
  (800) 424-9346
  http://www.epa.gov/epaoswer/hotline
- **Safe Drinking Water Hotline**
  (800) 426-4791
  http://www.epa.gov/safewater
- **U.S. Department of Housing and Urban Development**
  http://www.hud.gov
- **EPA Indoor Air Quality**—Links to Other Agencies
  http://www.epa.gov/iaq/moreinfo.html
- **Centers for Disease Control and Prevention**
  http://www.cdc.gov/
- **The Schnapf Environmental Law Center**
  Although private, provides simple explanations of many environmental issues
  http://www.environmental-law.net/

case study

Tandy McIntyre represents Carl Jurgensen, a prospective buyer looking for a home in Bloomington, Indiana. Carl is moving from Minnesota and, as far as Tandy knows, never had his home tested for any environmental hazards. He has not expressed any concerns to Tandy about environmental issues.

Tandy has found a listing that would be ideal for Carl. When she calls him to describe the home, he is ecstatic. He wants to buy now. The property is near the university's rather large power plant. Tandy is not aware of any environmental problems in the area associated with the power plant. She has not talked to any neighbors, nor has she asked Carl about his attitudes toward environmental issues. She does not tell Carl about the power plant because he has never indicated that could be a problem.

1. The best way for Tandy to avoid trouble with environmental issues is to
   a. raise issues but let clients make their own assessment of environmental hazards.
   b. rely on the seller's property disclosure form.
   c. get all the facts before disclosing information about environmental hazards.
   d. provide information and advice to her client on her own initiative.

2. Which of the following environmental problems probably would not be a high priority for a residential real estate agent?
   a. Asbestos
   b. Chipping and peeling paint in an old house
   c. Toxic waste sites
   d. Indoor air pollution

Student Comments

Please provide your comments regarding the basic principle(s) addressed in this case study, and its relevance to the subject matter generally:

_____

_____

_____

_____

Chapter 1 Review Questions

1. When is the ideal time to raise environmental issues with a buyer?
   a. At the first interview
   b. Only if mentioned on the property disclosure form
   c. Prior to closing (escrow)
   d. After closing (escrow)

2. The law that prompted environmental disclosures in a residential real estate transaction was
   a. caveat emptor.
   b. the Clean Air Act of 1970.
   c. the Lead-Based Paint Hazardous Reduction Act (LBPHRA).
   d. the Toxic Substance Control Act (TSCA).

3. Of the following environmental hazards, residential buyers are most likely to be concerned about
   a. wetlands.
   b. toxic waste sites.
   c. underground storage tanks.
   d. lead-based paint.

4. In the past, sellers usually disclosed only structural defects. Of the following, buyers are now realistically expecting disclosure of
   a. county plans for the area.
   b. environmental issues.
   c. seller's plans for reinvesting their equity.
   d. building permits that might be required for any renovation.

5. A truly effective real estate licensee should expect to
   a. be an environmental issues expert.
   b. offer advice on whether or not to test.
   c. ignore questions about environmental issues.
   d. provide information where the consumer can find additional resources in order to make an informed decision.

6. Residential seller property disclosure forms can be viewed as
   a. a guarantee that all is okay.
   b. a warranty that the seller will repair or clean up any problems.
   c. yet another useless form to sign.
   d. a starting point from which the buyer can decide to test or not.

7. The first step in reducing environmental risk in the real estate transaction is to
   a. learn the basics of environmental hazards.
   b. ignore questions unless they have been raised at least twice.
   c. suggest that buyers test for every hazard mentioned in this book.
   d. not worry consumers since they have hired the real estate licensee to handle all of the details.

8. Which of the following is the best place to begin to learn more about environmental issues?
   a. Environmental Law Institute
   b. U.S. Department of Housing and Urban Development
   c. Department of Energy
   d. Environmental Protection Agency

9. Some states require that a licensee ask additional questions because of the doctrine of
   a. caveat emptor.
   b. "should have known."
   c. seller beware.
   d. see nothing, hear nothing, say nothing.

10. Full disclosure of environmental issues permits buyers
    a. to rely on sellers for repairs and/or removal.
    b. to avoid having to pay for any tests themselves.
    c. to negotiate on a level playing field with the sellers.
    d. and their agents to rely on seller-supplied disclosure forms.

part B
Indoor Environmental Issues

chapter two

Lead-Based Paint

learning objectives

Upon completing this chapter, you will be able to

- explain what lead is and identify the major health hazards of lead.
- discuss how children ingest lead and why children are more vulnerable than adults.
- list three ways to test for the presence of lead in the home.
- explain at least three ways to clean up lead-based paint.
- list five basic requirements sellers/landlords must perform in order to comply with federal law.
- name at least three penalties for noncompliance.
- summarize areas of concern that contingencies should cover in the sales contract.

■ Key Terms

chelation	LBPHRA	target housing
chemical spot test	lead blood level	X-ray fluorescence
encapsulation	lead poisoning	

■ What Is Lead?

Lead is a heavy, soft, malleable, blue-gray metal found either as a natural ore or a by-product of smelting silver. In its natural state (see Figure 2.1), lead is not a problem. Once processed, however, it is part of the environment forever. There is no known way to dispose of lead nor a method to render lead harmless.

Easy to find and easy to manipulate, lead has been used continuously and extensively for more than seven centuries. Some historians have suggested that the decline of the Roman Empire was brought on by undetected lead poisoning.

Figure 2.1 | Galena Ore

Source: U.S. Geological Survey

Greeks determined that lead was a poison, and even today, some folk medicines still contain lead. In a recent study of South Asian grocery stores in Boston, Dr. Robert B. Saper found that one in five herbal medicine products made in India and Pakistan contained potentially harmful levels of lead.

From the beginning of the Industrial Revolution through the end of World War II, lead usage intensified. During this time, lead was found in just about all aspects of daily life: electrical storage batteries, ammunition, gasoline, wooden window weights, building construction, roofing cornices, solder in electrical conduit, and water and sewer pipes. Its most extensive use was as a pigment in paints, and sometimes in varnishes and primers. Today we live with that legacy.

■ What Are the Effects of Lead in the Human Body?

Lead poisoning occurs when high concentrations of lead are ingested either by mouth or from breathing fine particles. Lead does not stay long in the bloodstream and ordinarily passes through the body in a few days. However, lead may become lodged in soft tissue and bone. It may also enter the brain where it can do serious and irreparable damage, especially to children.

Early symptoms of excessive levels of lead in adults include irritability and restlessness, vomiting, and drowsiness. Prolonged exposure can destroy blood cells, induce anemia and hypertension, trigger gallbladder problems or appendicitis, and cause reproductive problems in both men and women. A more insidious condition is chronic lead poisoning, a result of accumulation of lead over a long period of time. Pregnancy, severe illness, or even osteoporosis can trigger the release of lead stored in the body and thus cause problems long after the initial exposure.

Children under the age of six are the most vulnerable to damage from lead for several reasons. First, they are more likely to ingest lead by putting hands and objects that might have lead dust on them into their mouths. Also, their absorption rate for lead is five times that of adults. Finally, their brains and nervous systems are in the formative stage and are thus more vulnerable to toxic attack. Excessive lead levels in children may cause brain damage and affect the nervous system, kidneys, hearing, and coordination. It can cause headaches and behavior problems and can affect learning. In extreme cases, it can cause blindness or death. The EPA estimates that one out of every 11 (more than 1.7 million) American children have elevated blood lead levels.

■ What Are the Sources of Lead Exposure?

Air—Very fine airborne particles are inhaled. Still other particles find their way into our mouths by settling on food or on objects placed into the mouth (toys, for example).

Lead in dust can come from chalking, weathering, and chipping of lead-based paint. Scraping or sanding during renovation helps spread the dust. Even raising and lowering old windows disturbs the paint and may cause the sash weights (usually made of lead) to release fine particles of lead. Lead dust accumulates and is easily carried by many sources: clothing, tools, pets, shoes, and so on.

Food—Today, the main source of lead in food comes from lead glazes on ceramics, pottery, and china. Even food grown in home gardens may contain lead from airborne particles found in the dust, a legacy of leaded gasoline.

Water—Although most water mains and plumbing lines constructed with lead have been replaced, lead is still found in some plumbing supplies including lead alloys in faucets (brass or bronze).

■ How Is Lead Poisoning Discovered?

Lead in the body is measured by a blood screen measurement and is expressed as micrograms per deciliter (μg/dl). The general population in the United States is now estimated to have a lead blood level of 2.8 μg/dl. This is down from a level of 26 μg/dl in the 1960s and 12.8 μg/dl in the late 1970s. The decline is largely a result of eliminating lead from gasoline. A blood test usually discloses recent exposure. Further testing is required to discover concentrations retained in bone or soft tissues, indicative of much earlier exposure.

It is a fallacy to think that children eat paint to supplement their diets and thus ingest lead. Parents and others bring lead indoors. Airborne lead can be widely spread through the use of an ordinary vacuum cleaner, landing on fingers, toys, and other household items that children touch, suck, or chew.

■ What Is the Treatment for Lead Poisoning?

According to the Center for Disease Control and Prevention, a child has lead poisoning when blood levels are above 15 μg/dl. A level over 45 μg/dl is considered a medical emergency and may require hospitalization. When elevated lead levels are found, testing is done to determine the source (home, day care, etc.) of the contamination so that appropriate measures can be taken to correct the cause.

Sometimes, simply the passage of time reduces lead levels within the body to an acceptable range, but the only way to quickly eliminate lead from the body is by chelation, a process whereby an ingested substance combines chemically with lead so that it can be excreted through the urinary system. There can be serious side effects from the treatment, so the best solution is to prevent contamination in the first place.

■ How Is Testing for the Presence of Lead Done?

Three types of tests are available to a property owner or specialist. Two of the methods, spot and scrape testing, produce many false negative and false positive results. Also, both create "spots" on the woodwork and the walls wherever testing has been done, and the property owner must then cover the blemishes. Unfortunately, only the third method is nondamaging, but it is costly. The three methods are:

1. **Chemical spot testing**—A solution is applied to a painted surface, which causes a chemical reaction. The test is quick and inexpensive but is not totally accurate. It determines the presence of lead but not the amount. It is also destructive because surface paint must be scraped to get to older, lower levels.

2. **Paint scrapings**—This method requires sending 30 to 70 chips of paint to a lab for chemical analysis. Again, this is destructive, potentially expensive, and slow since it takes the lab several days to process the chips.
3. **X-ray fluorescence**—The only truly accurate and nondestructive method for determining lead concentration levels requires the use of an expensive X-ray instrument. The machine bombards a sample with X-rays. This causes lead ions to become excited and decay. The emitted particles are measured in milligrams per square centimeter (mg/cm^2). Although testing can be done on-site, the operator must be experienced to ensure the most accuracy.

■ Can Lead-Based Paint Be Cleaned Up?

There are five ways to safely eliminate a problem due to lead-based paint.

1. **Replacement**—Perhaps the easiest and least costly method is to simply replace old doors, windows, trim, and other woodwork with new materials.
2. **Encapsulation**—Covering lead paint may be done with wood, vinyl, aluminum, tile, stone, drywall, plaster, and special coatings. The area must be prepared by wet scraping and seams must be sealed after the surface is encapsulated.
3. **Off-site chemical stripping**—Messy and expensive, this is one way to preserve decorative woodwork. Wood trim is removed from the house and stripped in a chemical solution.
4. **Wet scraping**—Of temporary limited use in areas where peeling paint is a problem, the paint is thoroughly wetted with a chemical solution and then scraped with a wire brush, paint scraper, or similar item. Thorough cleanup is necessary, and the liquid waste must be properly disposed of.
5. **Heat guns**—These are effective and are often used to soften thick paint prior to scraping. Unfortunately, lead may be vaporized; thus, special care must be taken when using a heat gun. The use of special respirators is strongly recommended.

■ What Efforts Have Been Made to Ban the Use of Lead?

By the end of World War II, public health officials became increasingly aware of the poisonous effects of lead on humans and pushed hard for reductions in lead usage. Eventually, this resulted in the banning of lead in gasoline in the early '70s and from paint in 1978.

At the present time, Title X of the Housing and Community Development Act of 1992, known as the Lead-Based Paint Hazard Reduction Act (LBPHRA), seeks to control exposure to lead-based paint hazards. Federal funds are available to assist states in developing training and certification programs for anyone providing testing or remediation services. The act is a major step for the federal government, as it represents the first time the government has become involved with residential real estate transfer, and it specifically mentions protecting children under the age of six.

■ What Are the Five Basic Requirements of the EPA's Regulations?

LBPHRA requires that sellers and their agents must do the following:

1. Disclose the presence of known lead-based paint and/or lead-based paint hazards in residential dwellings built before 1978.
2. Give buyers and tenants copies of any available reports dealing with the presence of lead-based paint or lead-based paint hazards.
3. Provide buyers and tenants with a federally approved lead-based paint hazard information pamphlet, "Protect Your Family from Lead in Your Home" *(for a copy, call (800) LEAD-FYI).*
4. Prior to entering into a purchase agreement, provide buyers (but not lessees) with a period of up to 10 days (or any time mutually agreed upon by buyer and seller) for the buyer to conduct a risk assessment or inspection to determine the presence of lead-based paint or lead-based paint hazards. The buyer may waive this testing opportunity.
5. Ensure that purchase agreements and leases include certain specified disclosures and acknowledgment language.

■ Who Must Comply with These Regulations?

The law puts the burden of compliance on sellers, lessors, and renovators, requiring them to disclose any prior test results or any actual knowledge of lead-based paint hazards. If a real estate licensee is involved, then the listing agent must advise sellers of their obligations to make the required disclosures. Any other agents involved in the transaction (subagent, buyer's agent, facilitator) are also responsible for seeing that the owners comply. The only agents who are exempt are buyer's agents who are paid entirely by the buyer.

Records should be kept for a minimum of three years for completed transactions.

REMEMBER: No one has to test; no one has to abate.

EPA Seeks Fines Totaling $730,000 in R.I. Lead Cases

The EPA is seeking $730,000 in civil penalties from three Rhode Island commercial property owners for repeat violations of lead-paint disclosure rules involving houses and apartments in four Rhode Island communities. Specifically, the violators failed to disclose lead hazards and/or to pass out lead-hazard information pamphlets.

According to the EPA the alleged violations occurred in low-income and minority neighborhoods, and many involved buildings occupied by families with young children. The EPA initiated its investigation after the state ordered four of the apartments to be cleaned up because significantly lead-poisoned children lived in them.

Source: *Peter B. Lord, Providence Journal, May 1, 2004*

Do These Regulations Apply to Owners of All Housing?

The regulations only apply to housing built prior to 1978 (target housing) with the following exceptions:

- Property sold at foreclosure, although the disclosure must be made at resale time
- Rental property that is certified "lead-based paint free" by an inspector who is certified under a federal program or federally authorized state certification program
- Property leased for 100 days or less, with no lease renewal or extension (i.e., most resort rental properties)
- Renewals of existing leases if disclosure was made at the time of the initial lease; disclosure must be made when renewing leases that were in effect on September 6, 1996
- Units with no bedrooms, no separation between sleeping and living areas (i.e., studio apartments, efficiencies, dormitories, military barracks, and individual rental rooms in residential dwellings)
- Housing for the elderly or disabled if children under the age of six are not expected to live there

How Can Agents Avoid Problems?

First, remember that target housing units are those built prior to 1978; thus, mandated disclosure of lead-based paint is not required in homes built after that date.

Second, agents should contact their local and state health departments to determine what resources are available to clients who wish to have a house tested. Health officials can more easily make suggestions as to whether or not a house poses potential problems to prospective buyers and their families. Agents should avoid offering suggestions or opinions about waiving the right to test or what would constitute adequate mitigation.

Since agents and sellers are required to disclose, an agent should discuss this law with sellers of homes built prior to 1978 as part of the listing presentation. It is possible that sellers have never considered lead as a hazard, and even with all of the publicity about the hazards of lead, many are totally unaware of the new law and its requirement of sellers.

It is useful to discuss lead-based paint very early on with buyer clients as part of the prequalifying interview, and to give the booklet to the buyer to read. For many buyers, there may be no problem at all.

However, families with small children may have more detailed questions and directions for the agent. It is better to learn at the beginning the buyers' attitudes toward and plans for older homes before showing any of them. Lead can be especially dangerous if airborne, a serious problem during remodeling, especially when children are present. If parents with small children are planning to do this, they should be informed of the dangers.

Finally, agents should be familiar with the proper disclosure forms and recognize what they disclose and require, as well as what they do not cover.

Remember that most agents get into trouble by assuming too much responsibility. For instance, buyers might ask if they should have the house tested for lead-based paint, and the agent, wishing to be helpful, might use the following inappropriate responses:

- *Don't worry about testing . . .*
- *I've lived in old houses, and I haven't had a problem.*
- *As long as you keep the kids off the floor . . .*
- *You don't have kids, so you don't have to worry.*
- *It's only a problem for low-income families.*
- *As long as you don't eat the paint (said with a chuckle) . . .*

More appropriate responses include:

- *Whether or not to test is a decision that I cannot make for you. Here is the number of the lead program official here in (state).*
- *Who to hire is a decision that I cannot make for you. Here is the number of the lead program official here in (state).*

■ Are There Penalties for Noncompliance?

Jail Time
Maryland, April 2004 (Baltimore Sun)

A Maryland property manager who owns several rental properties in Baltimore was sentenced to 10 days in jail after ignoring numerous orders to remove lead from one of his properties.

★★★

Civil penalties can range up to $11,000 for each violation, i.e., each portion of the disclosure that is incomplete or incorrectly filled out. Those who intentionally violate the law can face up to one year imprisonment and much more in fines, or both. Injured parties can seek relief from both the federal statutes and state law for failure to disclose a hazardous condition, i.e., a material defect.

The injured purchaser or lessee may receive up to three times the damages sustained. Such damages may include the costs of correcting the lead-based paint hazards and medical costs related to lead-based paint poisoning.

■ What about the Disclosure Forms?

Sellers and lessors must make all disclosures mentioned, but only to the actual purchaser/lessee. The actual buyer then has up to ten days to have the testing done, or the buyer may waive the right to test.

Although no one is required to test or abate for lead, disclosure forms are required and must contain the following:

1. Lead warning language exactly as written in the EPA form
2. Seller/lessor acknowledgment of disclosure of known lead-based paint
3. Purchaser/lessee acknowledgment of receiving the required disclosures and receiving the information pamphlet

4. Purchaser acknowledgment that he or she has a ten-day period to test or may agree to a shorter time frame or to waive the right altogether
5. Agent acknowledgment that he or she has advised the seller/lessor of his or her obligations and that agent understands his or her responsibility to ensure that the seller/lessor complies with the disclosure requirements
6. Certification by all parties of the accuracy of the information received

Note that the burden of disclosure is on the seller/landlord as well as renovators. Agents are cautioned to remain neutral in their presentation of the form, all the while advocating full disclosure. Even in the case of certain oral leases, the disclosure acknowledgment form must still be completed.

Many buyer's agents have found it helpful to discuss the forms very early in their relationship with buyers. These questions are not required by law but they can identify important issues and help in their resolution.

Useful questions to buyers include:

- *Will you ask to have the home tested? If so, whom will you use?*
- *Are you looking for a totally lead-free home? If not, what conditions are you willing to accept?*
- *What level of abatement are you willing to accept?*

Is This All There Is?

A selling (buyer's) agent should make sure that the listing agent has advised the seller of his or her obligation. The listing agent should confirm that the selling agent has given the pamphlet to the purchaser. Both agents should make sure that the offer includes the Disclosure of Information and Acknowledgment form. Only agents paid entirely by the buyer and representing the buyer are exempt.

What Is the Effect of Disclosure or Testing on Contracts?

Although federal law requires disclosure of lead-based paint hazards, it does not specify what is to be done after disclosure is made. It is thus left to real estate professionals to handle the many questions typically raised by testing and disclosure. Normally this is done by incorporating contingency clauses in written sales agreements.

Unfortunately, there are no federal guidelines for contingency wording. Agents should determine their buyers' attitudes toward testing and then discuss all possibilities, the "what-ifs." Contingencies that fit the needs and circumstances for each individual situation should be written. Here are some areas of concern that well-written contingencies should clarify:

- Since any time frame may be agreed upon, it is best to have a beginning and ending time for the testing period.
- The purchaser may decide to have the home tested even if the seller already has done so.

- A contingency should discuss a specific lead level which is (or is not) acceptable to the buyer. Verbiage such as "Unacceptable levels of lead-based paint" is ambiguous and open to interpretation.
- Does the buyer have the right to rescind the contract should specified lead levels be exceeded? If so, the period of rescission should be clearly stated.
- What happens to the earnest money if the contract is voided?
- Can a seller continue to receive and accept other offers during the testing period?
- Does the seller have the option of abatement? Within what time frame? Up to what cost?
- Whose responsibility is it to clean up the house after lead has been removed?

Where Can I Get More Information?

State and local health departments normally have information about certified testers and contractors. State phone numbers can be found in the last few pages of "Protect Your Family from Lead in Your Home." HUD's "Lead Listing" provides monthly updates of trained and approved lead inspectors, risk assessors, and abatement contractors. Additional sources include:

- **National Lead Information Center**
  (800) 424-LEAD
  http://www.nsc.org/ehc/lead.htm
- **Housing and Urban Development "Lead Listing"**
  (888) 532-3547
  http://www.leadlisting.org/
- **Office of Healthy Homes and Lead Hazard Control**
  U.S. Dept. of Housing and Urban Development
  451 Seventh Street SW, B-133
  Washington, DC 20410
  http://www.hud.gov/offices/lead/index.cfm

case study

Horace and Denise Granatos have two infant children. They need to move from their apartment in Philadelphia to a house, but can only afford one of the city's older homes. They have heard a lot of stories about children dying after eating lead-based paint from the walls in old homes, and they are worried about it happening to their two children.

They have contacted Penn Country Realty, a small brokerage one of their friends used to buy a home. They told their agent, Sandy Allenton, about their concerns related to lead-based paint. They also told him they don't know anything about identifying or fixing lead-based paint problems. Within a week Sandy was able to show them a modest home that met their needs and budget. The home needed some work, but basically was in good shape. The first question they asked Sandy is whether they should have the house tested for lead-based paint.

1. The most appropriate response for Sandy to give to the Granatos family about whether they should test for lead-based paint is
   a. the seller is responsible for that decision.
   b. only if buyers have family history of lead-based paint health problems.
   c. the local government is responsible for that decision.
   d. buyers must make that decision themselves.

2. Often, the easiest way to safely eliminate a problem due to lead-based paint is
   a. replacement.
   b. x-ray fluorescence.
   c. heat guns.
   d. encapsulation.

Student Comments

Please provide your comments regarding the basic principle(s) addressed in this case study, and its relevance to the subject matter generally:

_____
_____
_____
_____

Chapter 2 Review Questions

1. Once lead has been removed from the ground and processed,
   a. it can never be rendered harmless.
   b. modern mitigation methods can render the lead harmless to humans.
   c. it is useless in the modern world.
   d. it can easily be disposed.

2. Who is most vulnerable to the effects of excessive lead levels in the blood?
   a. Baby boomers
   b. Seniors
   c. Children under the age of six
   d. It is equally toxic to all

3. How is lead poisoning discovered?
   a. X-ray fluorescence device
   b. Chemical spot testing
   c. Blood screen measurement
   d. Urinalysis

4. If the blood lead level is especially high, the only way to quickly reduce the level is through
   a. marking time and drinking lots of water.
   b. chelation.
   c. inoculation.
   d. quarantining the patient.

5. Which of the following is the easiest and least costly method to eliminate a lead-based paint problem?
   a. Off-site chemical stripping
   b. Wet scraping
   c. Heat guns
   d. Replacement

6. The Lead-Based Paint Disclosures apply to all of the following EXCEPT
   a. the seller of a house built in 1960.
   b. the owner of an apartment building built in 1940.
   c. the agent representing a seller of a 1960-built property.
   d. managers of studio apartments and dormitories.

7. When asked by the buyers, "Should we test for lead?" the licensee should respond
   a. "Whether or not to test is a decision that I cannot make for you."
   b. "Don't worry about testing. I've lived in a house like this for years and have had no problems."
   c. "Yes, you should test because that is the only way for you to know for sure."
   d. "It is too difficult and expensive to find a qualified tester, so keep the kids off the floor."

8. Are there any penalties for a violation of the Lead-Based Paint Hazard Reduction Act (LBPHRA)?
   a. Not sure, it is being challenged in the courts
   b. No, the law is a suggestion for disclosure
   c. Yes, but the penalties are minor
   d. Yes, expensive fines and/or imprisonment

9. An owner of a residential property never had the house that was built in 1940 tested for lead. Now that he is putting the house on the market, what should he indicate on the disclosure form?
   a. There is no lead-based paint.
   b. I have no knowledge of lead-based paint.
   c. Yes, there is lead-based paint because it was built in 1940.
   d. He should refuse to sign the disclosure.

10. Who of the following is required to make a disclosure regarding lead-based paint?
    a. Seller of a house built in 2002
    b. Landlord of an apartment building built in 1980
    c. Licensee who owns only one rental house purchased in 1976
    d. Renovator of an office building

chapter three

Radon

learning objectives

Upon completing this chapter, you will be able to

- define radon and describe the major health effects of exposure to radon.
- explain how radon enters buildings and why levels vary from house to house.
- define and explain the EPA's "action" level.
- describe the basic method of remediation and its cost range.
- determine when to discuss the subject of radon with buyers and sellers using your state's disclosure form.

■ Key Terms

action level	mitigation method	stack effect
carcinogen	picocuries	subslab suction
decay life	radon	

■ What Is Radon?

Radon is a naturally occurring, odorless, colorless, radioactive gas produced by the decay of uranium and radium, which can be produced in many different types of soils and rocks. Since radon is chemically inactive and not bound to other materials, it can move easily through pores or voids in soil, including soils found beneath homes.

■ How Does Radon Become a Health Hazard?

The half-life of radon is only 3.8 days. Radon gas decays into other radioactive decay products (RDPs), and these solid particles suspended in the air pose the greatest health risk. A few inhaled RDPs may adhere to lung tissue, emitting energy that can kill or damage sensitive cells and damage DNA molecules. Damaged DNA can produce DNA mutations, possibly leading to precancerous cells in the lungs.

Is There a Safe Level?

Figure 3.1 | How Does Radon Get Into a Building?

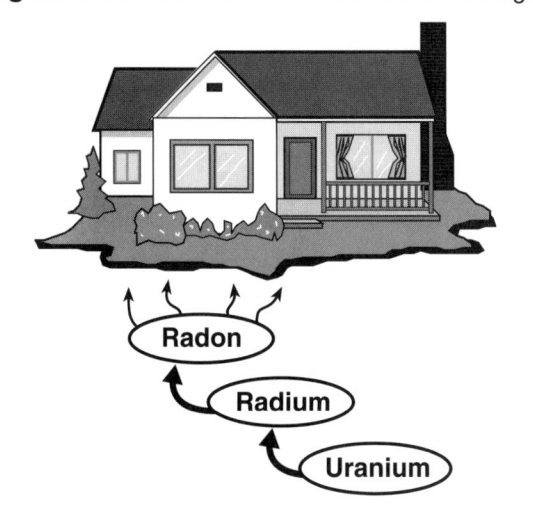

Radon is measured in picocuries (a unit of radiation) contained in a liter of air and is written as pCi/L. Since neither the EPA nor current scientific consensus has been able to establish a "threshold" safe level of radon exposure, minimizing exposure to radon is the recommended course of action.

Since there is no agreed-upon threshold, agents should avoid the phrase "safe level" or "safe readings." Instead, the Environmental Protection Agency (EPA) suggests an "action level" of 4 pCi/L; in other words, if a reading of four or higher is obtained, mitigation is suggested. An action level of 4 pCi/L was chosen because the EPA found that 95 percent of the time, current technology can economically reduce high radon levels in a home to levels below 4 pCi/L. In fact, 75 percent of the time, it can be reduced to 2 pCi/L.

Is Radon a Carcinogen?

The World Health Organization (WHO), the U.S. Department of Health and Human Services, and the EPA have all classified radon as a "Class A" known human carcinogen (along with cigarette smoke, benzene, and asbestos). With more than 50 years of worldwide studies, the health risks of radon are better known than most other human carcinogens. All of the studies have shown that the potential for developing lung cancer from radon exposure is a function of how much radon one is exposed to and for how long.

The largest and most extensive study was led by the National Cancer Institute (NCI), which examined the data on 68,000 underground miners who were exposed to a wide range of radon levels. The studies of miners are very useful because the subjects are humans, not rats, as in many cancer research studies. These miners are dying of lung cancer at five times the rate expected for the general population.

Table 3.1 | Recent North America Miner Studies

Ontario Uranium Miners	1984–1988
New Mexico Uranium Miners	1991
Radford & St. Clair Renard 1984	1988
Colorado Plateau Uranium Miners	1985–1988
Eldorado (Beaverlodge) Uranium Miners	1984–1986

How Does Radon Compare to Other Cancer-Causing Substances?

The EPA estimates annual deaths resulting from various causes are as follows:

- Pesticide application   100
- Hazardous waste sites   1,100
- Toxic outside air   2,000
- Pesticide residues on food   6,000
- Radon-induced lung cancers*   14,000

* With an uncertainty range of 7,000 to 30,000 deaths per year

Are Smokers Affected Differently?

Smoking GREATLY increases the risk of contracting lung cancer from radon.

- Not everyone who smokes gets lung cancer and some nonsmokers get lung cancer. However, smokers have a risk factor 15 times greater than nonsmokers.
- Being exposed to a lifetime of 4 pCi/L, two nonsmokers in 1,000 risk contracting lung cancer. A smoker in the same environment faces a significantly higher risk, 29 per 1,000.

Perceived Risk Versus Actual Risk

Fires claim very few lives in comparison to other causes, yet smoke detectors and fire alarms are mandatory in many buildings. When looking at causes of death, some events create greater perceptions of risk because of their sensational nature, such as plane crashes, bombings, fires, and storms. Radon claims more lives than drownings, fires, and airline crashes combined.

How Does Radon Get into a Building?

Thermal "stack effects" are caused by the natural upward movement of warm air in a home, creating positive pressures in upper areas (and escaping air) and negative pressures in the foundation areas where replacement air enters. Thus, a house acts like a vacuum, drawing soil gas, with radon, inside through cracks in concrete floors, openings around pipes and sump pumps, cracks in foundation walls, and so on. Kitchen and bath fans and the fans of heating systems accelerate this process.

Where Is Radon Found in the United States?

Radon is found everywhere. As a point of reference, radon levels in the outdoor air average 0.4 pCi/L.

Forty-two states and six Indian lands have conducted measurements in over 63,000 homes that estimate levels for 29 million homes. In addition, the EPA conducted the National Residential Radon Survey of 6,000 randomly selected homes that are statistically representative of all residential structures across the United States. These studies reached the following conclusions:

Figure 3.2 | Forces Drawing Radon into a Building

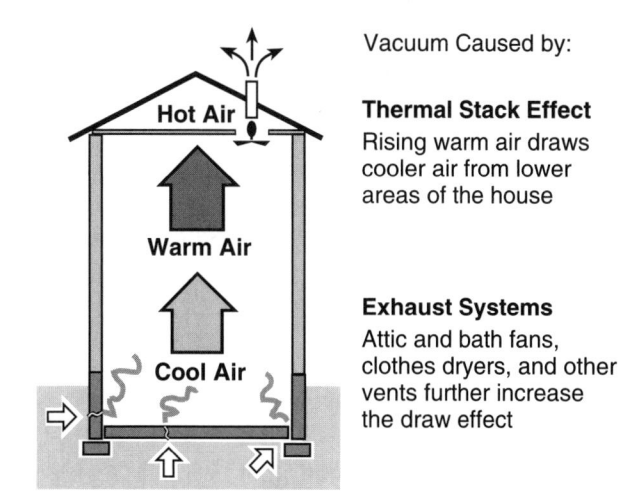

Vacuum Caused by:

Thermal Stack Effect
Rising warm air draws cooler air from lower areas of the house

Exhaust Systems
Attic and bath fans, clothes dryers, and other vents further increase the draw effect

- Radon levels above 4 pCi/L were found in every state.
- One out of 15 homes requires mitigation.

It is important to remember that radon levels can vary widely from building to building. The amount of radon moving through the soil entering a home can be affected by the strength of the radon source, soil type, water content of the soil, and void spaces in the soil.

Elevated radon levels have been found in every state. So, the only way to know whether a particular building has elevated radon levels is to test that building.

■ How Long Does Testing Take?

While a long-term test provides the best estimate of annual average radon levels, the required 90-day testing periods are not acceptable for most real estate sales situations. Accordingly, the EPA developed a shortened procedure that can be used to make home mitigation decisions. Their analysis showed that about 94% of the time, a 48-hour test satisfactorily predicts whether a home's annual average is at or above 4 pCi/L.

If a passive test device is used, results are normally received within ten days to two weeks. When a continuous monitor is used, results are available immediately.

■ What Testing Devices Are Used?

Testing devices are usually classified as either passive (i.e., requiring no power or operator) or active.

1. **Passive devices** are usually small bottle-like collection canisters with a removable seal or cap that is used to activate the test. They include alpha track detectors, charcoal canisters, charcoal liquid scintillation detectors, and

electron ion chambers. Detectors available for homeowner use typically cost from $20 to $30, which includes the test evaluation fee. Look for labeling saying "Meets EPA Requirements," "EPA Listed," or "EPA Approved."

2. **Active devices** include different types of continuous monitors. They require electrical power, and usually a trained technician. Testing by professional companies typically costs about $75, but with more sophisticated equipment, the cost can range from $100 to $150.

If a 48-hour continuous device is used, the EPA indicates that only one test need be done in a real estate transaction. All real estate testing should be done at the lowest level of the home that is "suitable for occupancy." This varies from family to family, depending on how the basement (if present) is used.

■ Who Does the Testing?

Prior to 1998, the EPA offered a Radon Proficiency Program (RPP) to certify radon testers. Certification is now handled primarily by two professional associations, the National Radon Safety Board (NRSB), and the National Environmental Health Association. Both have Web sites that describe their programs and provide lists of experts by region. (See "Where Can I Get More Information" later in this chapter). Licensees and consumers should rely only on radon testing services certified by one of these associations.

■ How Is Test Tampering Prevented?

The best way to prevent tampering is to use professionally trained testers. Since private residential testing is normally performed unattended, it is difficult for untrained personnel to detect tampering. However, testers must follow specific test protocols to ensure accurate results and are trained to look for suspicious results. Also, if the need arises, they will go to court to back their tests.

> **A TRUE STORY**
>
> A tester in Iowa believed there had been seller tampering during his first test. On the retest, he returned to the home four hours early, but was unable to find the test device. Upon searching he found the canister in the homeowner's freezer!

■ Tips for Good Measurements

The test device should be placed at least 20 inches off the floor, in the lowest level that is suitable for occupancy. In most cases, sellers will not know how a buyer might use the home. If a lower area of the home could be used regularly as a family/living room, playroom, den, or bedroom, test there. In addition, testers should:

- **Avoid drafts**—Testing should be done with windows and doors closed, except for normal entering and exiting. Also, try not to operate exhaust fans or operate air conditioners that bring in fresh air.

- **Avoid kitchens and baths**—Hot spots and the humidity of kitchens and baths adversely affect results.

- **Avoid weather extremes**—It is not useful to test during periods of severe storms or high winds. The low pressure of storms and winds can substantially affect radon entry rates into a home.

- **48-hour minimum**—Most home testing devices specify an exact exposure duration. In no case should this be less than 48 hours.

Can Homes Be Fixed?

Definitely, yes! Mitigation methods consist primarily of active soil depressurization (subslab suction) to remove radon gas before it seeps into the house. Usually, a hole is drilled in the concrete slab or basement floor, and a 4" PVC pipe is routed up through walls and closets to the attic. A fan installed in the pipe "sucks" air upward and vents it outside the home (see Figure 3.3).

Nationwide, typical installation time is one to two days with total costs ranging from $600 to $1,500 depending on region and the type of system installed. If a radon mitigation system is included as part of new home construction, the cost is much lower, averaging $300 to $400. Operating costs run $75 to $175 annually and include power for a fan and any heated/cooled air losses from the home.

To keep everyone honest, an independent tester, not the mitigation contractor, should make follow-up radon testing 24 hours after repairs have been made. For assistance, call the state radiation control official, health department, or office of environmental protection.

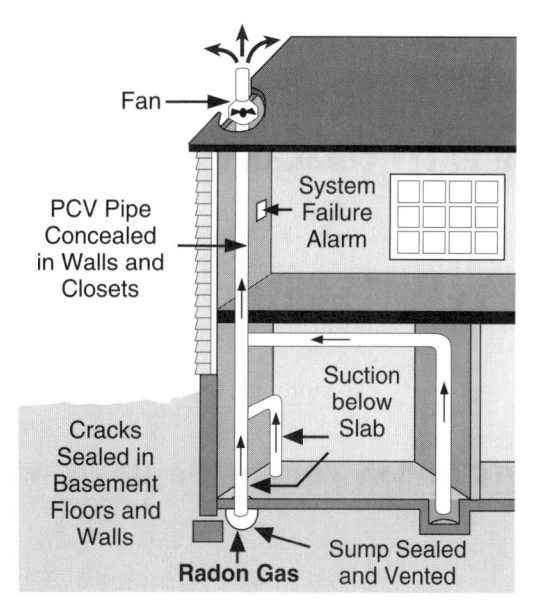

Figure 3.3 | Subslab Suction

Who Does Repairs?

At one time, the EPA offered programs certifying for radon inspectors and mitigators. In 1998, the EPA discontinued these certification programs in favor of private contractors. However, the EPA still endorses mitigation standards provided by the American Society for Testing and Materials (ASTM). These standards are available on the EPA Web site until 2006, and thereafter can be purchased from ASTM.

Several professional organizations offer certification programs, including the National Radon Safety Board (NRSB) and the National Environmental Health Association. Both have Web sites that describe their programs and provide lists of experts by region ("Where Can I Get More Information" below). Homeowners should get at least two estimates, research references, and compare prices, as they would for any home repair.

Can New Homes Be Constructed that are Radon-Resistant?

Yes, this is the best time to test and install abatement devices. Estimated costs for materials and labor range from $350 to $500 versus retrofitting an existing home for $800 to $2,500. Mitigation during construction improves energy efficiency and typically costs between $200 and $300.

The following organizations have developed model building standards and codes for building radon-resistant homes.

- **National Association of Home Builders**
  http://www.nahb.org/
  type "Radon" into the search window that appears
- **American Society for Testing and Materials,**
  ASTM Standard WK2469 Guide for Radon Control Options for the Design and Construction of New Low Rise Residential Buildings
  http://www.astm.org/
- **Environmental Protection Agency,**
  Model Construction Standard (EPA 402R-94-009)
  http://www.epa.gov/radon/pubs/newconst.html

Can Radon Enter Through the Water Supply?

Yes, although compared to radon entering a home through soil, entrance through water is a small source of risk. Radon can be released through showerheads into the air and through other household uses of water. The solution is to remove the radon before it enters a home.

For more information, call the EPA's Water Hotline number: (800) 426-4791.

How Should Radon Testing Be Dealt with in Real Estate Sales?

The key to a successful closing involves timely and reliable testing to determine the radon potential. Ideally, the test is done using an independent third party who can properly interpret the results and who will safeguard against tampering. It should be performed early enough in the transaction to allow time for mitigation, if called for.

■ What about Property Disclosure Forms?

More than 35 states require or suggest disclosure of known radon levels. Most of the time, unless they have tested for radon, property owners indicate "unknown." Therefore, buyers should be cautioned not to rely too much on the disclosure forms as a guarantee that there are no problems.

Many times, the forms lead to additional questions. Real estate licensees can be helpful to clients and customers by handing out informational brochures and understanding mitigation techniques so they can educate their clients and customers about the issues and problems raised in the disclosure forms.

The buyer's agent should try to determine the buyer's attitude about radon and should discuss not only testing but also mitigation methods to bring the reading to below the action level of 4. It is wiser to discuss these issues before buyers see the house of their dreams.

■ What Should Agents Avoid Saying?

Watch out for these remarks; they won't sound good in front of a jury!

- *"The house tested safe before."*
- *"There is no radon in the home."*
- *"I never heard of radon being a problem in this neighborhood."*
- *"I know an agent who had a house tested down the street last year, and it was okay."*
- *"Let's see if we can get you a safe reading."*
- *"The only people concerned about radon are relocation companies. We don't have any relocating buyers; there is no need to worry."*

With buyers, it is BETTER for the agent to use statements like the following:

- *"Radon can be a concern in this neighborhood as well as any other area. It varies from house to house."*
- *"You may want to discuss a radon test with a state health official or a certified tester. Here are phone numbers for . . ."*
- *"Here are some booklets to read that may help you decide."*

■ Where Can I Get More Information?

- For a wealth of general information about radon visit the **EPA Radon Web site**: *http://www.epa.gov/iaq/radon/*
- The EPA offers a short **Radon Educational Video** on how best to handle radon in residential real estate transactions. With a bit of light humor, the video covers the basics on a wide range of radon topics. The primary audiences are homebuyers and sellers, and real estate sales agents and brokers. Single copies of the video are free from IAQ-INFO, (800) 438-4318, in VHS, CD, and DVD formats.

- The **Centers for Disease Control** offer detailed information about radon health issues. The CDC can also be reached by phone at (888) 422-8737 or by e-mail at *ATSDRIC@cdc.gov,* or on the Web at *http://www.atsdr.cdc.gov/tfacts145.html.*
- Use the **EPA State Expert Locator** Web page to locate the nearest radon expert in your region: *http://www.epa.gov/iaq/whereyoulive.html*
- **Mitigation Standards** endorsed by the EPA and ASTM are available at *http://www.epa.gov/radon/pubs/mitstds.html*
- **National Radon Safety Board** *http://www.nrsb.org/*
- **National Environmental Health Association** *http://www.radongas.org/*

case study

Sol Ordoñez is negotiating the purchase of a home in Toledo, Ohio, for the Wells family. He has received the seller's property disclosure form. When he shows the form to his clients, they notice that the answer to the question about radon levels is "unknown." They ask Sol if he thinks the home is safe.

Sol checks with his colleagues, who say that other homes in the neighborhood that have been tested for radon have shown levels below the EPA's "action level." Sol notifies the Wells family that "radon is not a problem in the neighborhood."

1. The best way to determine if a home has high radon levels is to
   a. test the home.
   b. check the property disclosure form.
   c. review the results of previous tests.
   d. consult the EPA's assessment of neighborhood levels of radon.

2. The EPA's radon exposure "action level" is the level of radon exposure at which the EPA
   a. requires radon exposure mitigation.
   b. declares a home unsafe.
   c. recommends radon exposure mitigation.
   d. requires real estate agents to disclose radon exposure levels.

Student Comments

Please provide your comments regarding the basic principle(s) addressed in this case study, and its relevance to the subject matter generally:

_____

_____

_____

_____

Chapter 3 Review Questions

1. What is radon?
   a. Inert gas produced by lead smelting plants
   b. By-product of industrial manufacturing
   c. Runoff produced by excessive use of agriculture fertilizers
   d. Naturally occurring radioactive gas

2. What is the EPA's position regarding radon testing and mitigation?
   a. Since radon is naturally occurring, there is no need to test or mitigate.
   b. A safe level of radon exists provided that the home is occupied by nonsmokers.
   c. Mitigation is recommended if the radon level is four or higher.
   d. Testing is required in certain states with higher levels.

3. Of the following tests, which is most practical in a real estate transaction?
   a. X-ray fluorescent device
   b. 90-day testing with electronic readings
   c. Passive device such as a charcoal canister
   d. 48-hour, continuous device

4. Generally, in the United States, radon is found
   a. only in mountainous states.
   b. in every state and territory.
   c. primarily in deep mines and not in residential structures.
   d. to be one of the primary causes of "sick building syndrome."

5. What is the first and easiest step in radon mitigation?
   a. Install PVC pipes from the basement to the attic
   b. Install a "whole-house" exhaust fan
   c. Seal cracks in basement floors and foundation walls
   d. Encapsulate the radon with a special substance to prevent it from becoming airborne

6. During construction, a new home can be
   a. fitted with radon abatement devices.
   b. sealed, but no radon abatement devices can be installed until radon is actually detected.
   c. secured against radon seeping in by reducing the number of exhaust fans in the home.
   d. protected from radon by the installation of a HEPA furnace/air conditioner.

7. Regarding radon, the real estate licensee can advise the buyer client to
   a. ignore any home that already has an installed radon mitigation system.
   b. include as a contingency in the offer, "contingent on a radon reading of 0."
   c. rely on the home inspector to indicate whether or not a test should be done.
   d. discuss the radon issue with someone from the state health department.

8. Of the following situations, when should the real estate licensee bring up the radon issue?
   a. Initial interview before showing any homes
   b. When the buyer is ready to make an offer on the home
   c. Between contract signing and closing (escrow)
   d. After the closing (escrow)

9. Of the following, where is the best place to place the radon testing device?
   a. Attic
   b. Master bedroom on second floor
   c. Living room on first floor
   d. Workout room in basement

10. After a mitigation system has been installed, who, if anyone, should perform the follow-up testing?
    a. Home inspector
    b. Installer of mitigation system
    c. Tester independent of the installer
    d. No one; systems work pretty well without added expense of testing

chapter four

Mold

learning objectives

Upon completing this chapter, you will be able to

- describe in general terms what molds are and name at least three conditions needed for them to grow.
- explain why mold has recently become a serious problem in real estate.
- describe at least five steps homeowners can take to reduce the potential for mold growth.
- discuss new construction factors that have impacted on mold-related health-problems.
- name several mold properties that can be harmful to humans.
- explain the difference between toxic and allergenic molds, and name at least two toxic molds occasionally found in homes.
- describe several major health risks of toxic molds and name the groups of people who are particularly vulnerable to them.
- describe remedial actions that should be taken for each of the three levels of mold contamination.

■ Key Terms

air exchanger	HEPA filters	mycotoxins
abatement	hyphae	spores
dirty-socks syndrome	infestation levels	stachybotrys
fungi	microbial VOCs	

■ Why Is Mold a Significant Issue for REALTORS®?

Mold hit the scene big-time in September 2001 when CBS did a *48 Hours* exposé entitled "Mold—the Silent Killers." The show chronicled the experiences of a

Texas family severely incapacitated by toxic mold who was awarded a $32 million judgment against their insurance company, since reduced to $4 million. *Newsweek* and *Time* magazines both have run cover stories on mold. It's even in Kansas! In 2002, the *Topeka Capitol Journal* ran a story on three Topeka homes with major mold infestations.

> **A TRUE STORY**
>
> Steve and Karen Porath purchased their home in California from the VA for $120,000 with $30,000 down and spent thousands more fixing it up. Two days after moving into the home, their newborn son began vomiting daily, sometimes more than 50 times a day.
>
> An engineering firm hired to conduct tests on the house confirmed that the house was contaminated with toxic stachybotrys mold. The Poraths' homeowners insurance company denied the estimated $75,000 mold removal claim. The VA said all homes are sold "as is."
>
> Sacramento County then condemned the infected home. The Poraths did not have the $75,000 needed to remediate the mold. The only choice left was to burn the house down and start over.
>
> Source: "Sick of Mold, They Torch Home" *Sacramento Bee*, February 15, 2001

These feature stories have raised public awareness of mold hazards. Individuals who previously might have suffered in silence now consider molds as a potential source of their mysterious illnesses.

Toxic mold is one of the recent health and environmental conditions of concern to homebuyers, homesellers, and real estate licensees. Like radon, asbestos, and lead paint, it is a potentially serious hazard in homes and a high-risk issue for real estate licensees. Mold is emerging as a major issue in real estate, but there are few guidelines for handling it.

■ Have Legal Actions Been Taken Against Real Estate Licensees?

Initially, lawsuits were brought against construction and insurance companies because they were perceived as having "deep pockets" with potential for large awards. Since then, insurance companies have amended their coverage to specifically exclude mold (and other environmental hazards). Consequently, litigants now target sellers, landlords, property management companies, and real estate licensees.

- **Renters v. Property Owners and Manager ($2.7m)**—*Mazza v. Shurtz*: In 2001, a California family won a $2.7 million personal mold injury suit against their apartment owners and property manager for ignoring the family's complaints regarding water intrusion and failing to properly maintain and repair their unit.
- **Buyer v. Listing Agent ($60k)**—A buyer, represented by his own buyer's agent, purchased a half-million dollar home in Phoenix, Arizona. At the suggestion of his agent, the buyer accepted a previous buyer's inspection report. During remodeling, a huge, virulent mold stain was uncovered. When the insurance company declined coverage, the buyer then sued the listing agent.

- **Renter v. Landlord ($1m)**—*New Haverford v. Stroot*: In 2001, the Delaware Supreme Court upheld a $1.04 million award to two women whose landlord failed to address leaks and mold problems in their apartments, resulting in serious health problems.

Why Are There So Many Mold Problems Recently?

Ironically, part of the reason for increased mold problems stems from an advance in construction technology and development of super-energy-efficient buildings. Newer construction materials also contribute to the problem. Even a change in American lifestyles has contributed to the problem.

- **Construction Techniques** —Homes in the last 10 to 15 years have been built airtight to conserve energy. If water leaks develop, there is little draft to dry out the water. Thus, once water gets inside, it stays trapped there. In the words of one industry consultant, "houses become giant petri dishes."
- **Construction Materials**— Drywall, particleboard, and pressed board all contain cellulosic components that provide a food source for the mold. These materials also tend to wick moisture into them if they are exposed to water through leaks or flooding.
- **Health and Lifestyle Factors**— It is estimated that Americans now spend 75 percent to 90 percent of time indoors. According to the EPA, indoor air quality in many buildings ranges from 10 to 200 times worse than ambient outdoor air. These airborne pollutants include chemicals released by household cleansers, synthetics, and construction materials. There are also many allergens including mites, dust particles, and mold spores. A sedentary, indoor lifestyle lowers the body's resistance to many pathogens, including molds. The increased exposure time to high levels of indoor allergens increases the number of people who become sensitized to them.

What Are Molds?

Molds are a type of fungi (pronounced fun-jee) similar to mushrooms that grow in filaments known as hyphae. These simple life forms lack the ability to photosynthesize, so they don't require sunlight to grow. Instead they use enzymes to digest nutrients from other organic materials, such as wallpaper and book collections. They are related to lichens and yeasts. There are more than 150,000 known species.

What Makes Molds Grow?

Mold needs four things to survive: moisture, a food source (usually cellulose, like an old book collection), oxygen, and warm temperatures. Most molds thrive in the presence of standing water or moisture levels above 65 percent. In homes, common food sources include wood, especially composites such as plywood and particle board, carpet backing, canvas, wallpaper, and paper.

Molds do not require light for growth, so they often go undetected, growing behind wallpaper, behind bath tiles, on carpet backing, and inside closets or other dark concealed areas. Homes with poor air circulation, water leaks, continued high humidity, and similar wet or moist conditions are especially prone to mold.

Many molds fluoresce under ultraviolet light. This unique trait can be used to help verify their presence in dimly lit areas.

How Does Mold Spread?

Molds often spread in round-shaped formations. This is due to the outward growth at the ends of the hyphae filaments. Mold usually has the appearance of a splotchy-looking layer on the surface of the food source. What is not apparent is that it also grows into the pores of the material to which it is attached. This is why surface scrubbing is usually an ineffective way to remove mold.

Is It Mold or Mildew?

When we see a patch or splotch of mold growing on closet wallpaper or smell our canvas camping tent stored in the basement, we often say it is "mildewed." Technically, this is an incorrect term. Mildew is a much less common, usually powdery life form that grows on plants. However, in laymen's terms we use the words interchangeably.

Why Do Molds Make People Ill?

- **Microbial VOCs**—Many molds release alcohols, ketones, and other hydrocarbons as they "digest" their food source. These are what cause the "musty" smell we associate with moldy places. Many people are allergic to the airborne MVOCs.
- **Spores**—Molds often release spores similar to pollens that cause allergic, respiratory, and sinus problems in some people. This can be very serious for some people, especially those with asthma or other respiratory illnesses.
- **Mycotoxins**—Under the right conditions, a few mold species produce poisons called mycotoxins. Unlike allergens, mycotoxins are toxic to virtually all people, and can be fatal to otherwise healthy people. They enter the body through inhalation, ingestion, or even skin contact. Some mycotoxins are so dangerous, they have been used to make weapons-grade nerve gas. It is the ability to produce mycotoxins that makes a mold a "toxic mold."

What Are Some of the More Toxic Molds?

- **Stachybotrys** (stack-ki-*bot*-triss)—"Stacky" for short, is the toxic mold most often reported in the news, notably in the previously mentioned toxic mold case in Texas. Stachybotrys is a slimy black mold rarely found indoors unless there has been major water intrusion due to flooding or sizeable leaks. It grows very quickly and needs a good food source and thus is typically found on drywall, ceiling tiles, and other materials containing paper or wood. It is not found on materials such as plastic, vinyl, or ceramic tiles, nor is it found on foods.
- **Other Toxic Molds**—Aspergillus (*ass*-per-jill-us) is a common species of indoor fungus that produces mycotoxins. Many also produce aflatoxins (*a*-flatoxins) which are carcinogenic in animals. Other toxic molds sometimes found in homes include fusarium (foo-*sair*-ree-um), penicillium (pen-ni-*sill*-lee-um, and paecilomyces (peh-sill-loh-*my*-cees).

What Are the Health Issues for Humans?

Humans react very differently from person to person, even within the same family. The symptoms can also be elusive. The most common problems are various allergenic responses, chronic sinusitis, and toxic effects.

Allergenic Effects

Allergic reactions to molds vary widely from person to person. Some may have no reaction while others may become severely ill. Two common allergens released by many molds are spores, which affect many people like pollens, and microbial VOCs (alcohols and ketones). Individuals may not be allergic to molds initially but may become hypersensitive to them after prolonged exposure to low levels over an extended period, or high level exposure for a shorter period. Common allergic reactions include:

- Allergic Rhinitis (cold symptoms)
- Asthma aggravation
- Dermatitis (red itchy skin blotches)
- Hypersensitivity Pneumonitis (pneumonia-like symptoms)

Chronic Sinusitis

Studies by the Mayo Clinic found that 93 percent of patients with chronic sinus infections actually had allergic fungal sinusitis. Previously, the prevailing medical opinion was that mold accounts for only 6 to 7 percent of all chronic sinusitis [*Newsweek*, December 4, 2000]. Additional studies are being done to confirm these findings.

Toxic Effects

Stachybotrys releases poisons that can cause internal bleeding in the lungs of infants and damage nerve cells in anyone. Experts believe it was used by the Soviets in the 1970s to produce biological weapons used in Cambodia and Afghanistan. Exposure to toxic mold can cause severe headaches, chronic fatigue, nose and throat irritation, persistent cold-like symptoms, and memory loss. In some cases, stachybotrys exposure can result in severe nerve and memory damage, lung hemorrhaging in infants, and even death.

Who is Most at Risk?

People with weakened immune systems, serious allergies, or severe asthma are more susceptible to lung infections or upper respiratory infections from mold exposure than most other people. Others most at risk are people whose immune systems are underdeveloped or have been weakened. These include the following:

- Infants, children, and elderly
- Immune-compromised persons
- HIV-infected persons
- Chemotherapy patients
- Patients with liver disease, etc.
- Pregnant women (fetus)
- Those with asthma and respiratory conditions

What Can People Do To Prevent Mold in Their Homes?

The easiest and most cost-effective way to prevent mold growth is to control moisture in the home. Basements are particularly susceptible so they should be checked periodically for signs of water intrusion. Make sure downspouts extend out from the house and that land grading slopes away from the house. Other simple measures include the following:

- Check windows, air conditioners, and humidifiers for leaks.
- Keep humidity level below 55 percent.
- Use an air conditioner or dehumidifier during humid months.
- Be sure there is adequate ventilation in kitchen and bathrooms.
- Use mold inhibitors, which can be added to paints.
- Do not carpet bathrooms.
- Remove and replace flooded carpets.

What about Filters and Air Exchangers?

Newer, energy-efficient homes are so tightly sealed that fresh air does not seep into the house. A device known as an air-to-air exchanger draws in fresh air from outdoors and passes it through a chamber that is surrounded by indoor air and then into the house. Stale moisture-laden indoor air is exhausted to the outside. Up to 80 percent of the heat can be recycled. More importantly, moisture levels inside the home are reduced during humid months, lowering the risk of mold growth. Many air exchangers are equipped with High Efficiency Particulate Acquisition filters (HEPA, pronounced hee-pa) that collect very small airborne particles including molds, spores, bacteria, dust, and mites. Ultraviolet air purifiers can be used to kill airborne molds, bacteria, and viruses.

Are There Tests To Find Mold in Homes?

There are three general methods of testing:

- Air sampling
- Surface lifting
- Destructive

Figure 4.1 | Air Exchanger

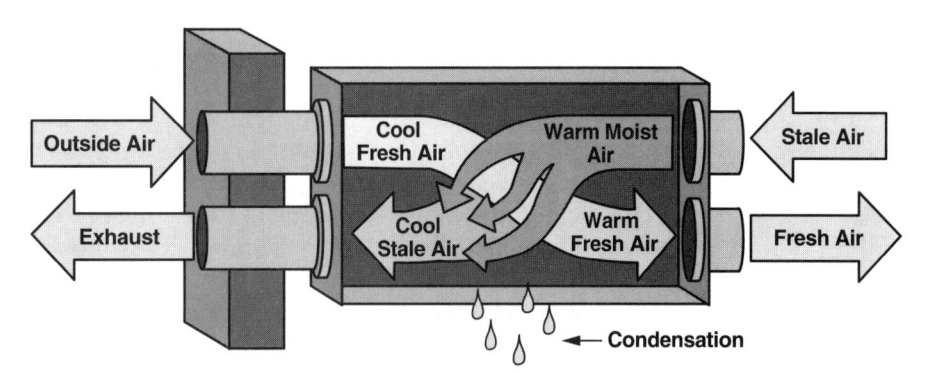

For molds that can be cultured, air is drawn across a plate coated with agar (a growing medium) for a specific amount of time. The spores are then incubated for several days and the number of colony-forming units (CFUs) are counted. For other molds, a spore trap method is used where air is pulled across a grease-coated slide for a specific period of time, then the number of spores are counted under a microscope. In both instances samples of outdoor air must also be tested and then compared to the indoor results. There is a problem when the indoor counts are higher than outdoor counts, or if there is a mold indoors that is different from outdoor molds.

Surface lifting tests use clear adhesive tape to lift mold samples from a contaminated surface. They must then be mailed to a certified tester. Care must be taken to avoid extra contamination.

Destructive tests are performed on contaminated materials, such as drywall, carpeting, and so on. They are removed from the premises and sent to a certified laboratory for testing.

■ Can Homeowners Do Testing Themselves?

Self-test kits are available in some home centers and on the Internet. These are a way to get a preliminary indication of mold infestation, but there is plenty of room for error in the hands of amateurs.

■ What about Professional Testing Services?

On-site testing services are quite expensive for use in most real estate transactions. Testing is often the best course of action when unexplained health problems occur or other mold tests indicate there may be a problem.

At the present time, there are no government standards or certifications. An Internet search indicates more than 100 organizations! None are perfect but most share requirements for certification that include work experience and coursework, ethical standards, and a method for revoking certification of individuals who do not adhere to those standards. Several of the more rigorous programs are sponsored by the following:

- Indoor Air Quality Association *(www.iaqa.org)*
- American Indoor Air Quality Council *(www.aiaqc.com)*
- Institute of Inspection Cleaning and Restoration *(www.iicrc.org)*

■ What Must Be Considered During Mold Abatement?

Mold abatement is more involved than one might think. For example, in smaller infestations, homeowners might be tempted to simply spray it with a biocide. However, simple drying may be sufficient without the hazardous effects that biocides might cause indoors. Biocides must be EPA-registered, and any application should strictly adhere to the product's printed instructions.

Another consideration is that mold often grows on both sides of building material, so if it is visible on the inside of the home, the outside or underside of the

Figure 4.2 | Mold Inside Closet from Wet Carpet

material should be examined. Mold may be the result of a water intrusion that may have occurred months or years earlier. All that is needed for the mold to literally mushroom in quantity is for the area to become wet again.

Interior spaces offer darkness and dampness. If growth is noted on wallpaper, for example, there may be growth inside the wall as well. Heat and air conditioning systems may be overlooked by non-HVAC people, but are often an area where major infestations take hold.

Mold infestations are categorized from one to five depending on the type of mold present and size of the contaminated area. The infestation level determines what actions to take as follows.

■ How Are Mold Infestations Cleaned Up?

First, amateurs should not attempt abatement. Done incorrectly, abatement can cause the spores to be spread through the home, and a simple problem can become complex. Second, without the proper precautions, amateurs can be overexposed and get sick themselves. The level of abatement also depends on the size and type of mold to be removed.

- **Level I** (10 sq. ft. or less)—Anyone removing Level I infestations should wear gloves, eye protection, and a disposable dust mask. Contaminated porous materials should be removed and sealed in bags to prevent further distribution of the spores. The contaminated areas and work areas should be thoroughly cleaned and dried.
- **Level II** (10 to 30 sq. ft.)—Level II infestations are handled much like Level I, but should be done by professionals.
- **Level III, IV, V** (more than 30 sq. ft.)—Homeowners should vacate the property when mold infestations exceed 30 square feet. Cleanup requires special contamination suits and equipment.

■ Why Do Many Older Homes Smell Like Mold?

Basements in older homes may have no drainage or vapor barriers; thus, the only way to prevent mold buildup may be constant dehumidification and/or removal of carpeting and wood paneling. Mold often grows in crawlspaces and dirt-floor cellars. Installing heavy plastic vapor barriers on dirt floors in cellars and crawlspaces is a way to minimize ground moisture penetration and mold growth. Older homes may have waterproof wall coverings or painted wallpaper that may cover hidden mold. Moisture may become trapped between this covering and the plaster underneath. For example, the fabric backing on wall covering (or original paper wallpaper) is an excellent food source for mold.

■ How Should Real Estate Licensees Handle Mold Issues?

Mold is now one of many environmental issues that impact real estate transactions on a regular basis. At this time, there are no federal requirements to disclose mold infestations, and only a few states require disclosure. It is unlikely that either state or federal standards will be issued in the near future. Several state REALTOR® associations include mold as part of their "standard" contracts.

Licensees must emphasize to buyers that sellers cannot disclose what they do not know. Buyers must be reminded that not only do they have the right to discover, they also have the burden to discover.

> **A TRUE STORY**
>
> When purchasing the $670,000 home in 2000, the buyers and sellers were so friendly that the buyers agreed to take the sellers' family dog "as their own treasured family pet for the rest of her natural life and to provide her original family liberal visitation as they wish." Prior to closing, the buyers had access to the house more than six times, noting a faint smell, but they also relied on the home inspection provided by the seller. As they moved in, they discovered plug-in air fresheners, cedar blocks in closets, and lava racks in a furnace vent and under a kitchen desk. Within weeks, all family members developed persistent headaches, nosebleeds, coughs, and other problems. Then they learned that the house had been "ozoned" four years earlier.
>
> The buyers sued for nondisclosure and the sellers contended that the buyers were negligent in not having their own inspection done. The judge felt that the buyers had an "opportunity to detect any odor before the sale." At the present time, the buyers are planning to burn the home and $193,600 in personal belongings. (Douglas County, NE District Court 1002383)
>
> Source: *Omaha World Herald*, January 25, 2004

The position of the National Association of REALTORS® on mold is: "Because this issue keeps growing, REALTORS® need to be aware of the concerns surrounding mold and may need to take steps to protect themselves from liability." Licensees should follow the risk reduction steps described in Chapter 1, namely, know the **B**asics, keep accurate **R**ecords, know the **E**xperts, **A**sk questions, and **D**isclose early and often.

Asking questions is particularly useful when dealing with mold, because unlike radon, often there are hints that it might be present. Ask further questions if anyone notices a musky odor or water stains on walls or ceilings. Sometimes dry mold stains or even active mold infestations can be seen. If anyone suspects a problem, they should ask about prior leaks, floods, and old damage.

Licensees and their clients should also recognize that testing for molds can be hazardous. Sellers do not want the testers to show up to test wearing a "space suit." However, testers must take precautions since repeated exposure can lead to problems, so sellers should be forewarned that the tester will wear protective coverings.

■ Where Can I Get More Information?

- The EPA's mold Web site is a well-organized hub with links to many sources of mold information: *http://www.epa.gov/iaq/molds*
- For additional information about health issues and mold, visit the **Centers for Disease Control** Web site: *http://www.cdc.gov/nceh/airpollution/mold*
- **The American Industrial Hygiene Association** mold resources Web page has numerous links to other organizations dealing with mold issues: *http://www.aiha.org/GovernmentAffairs-PR/html/prmoldsources.htm*
- **Clemson University (SC)** offers "Home Management Checklist: Preventing Home Moisture Damage" at: *http://virtual.clemson.edu/groups/psapublishing/PAGES/FYD/HL235.pdf*

case study

Last week, Mr. and Mrs. Byrd approached Sarah Johnson to ask for her assistance in locating a new home for them. The Byrds explained that they are both highly sensitive to pollen and, apparently, to some molds. Mrs. Byrd is the most sensitive and has been taken to the emergency room on several occasions with severe breathing difficulties. They inform Sarah that they intend to make their offer "contingent on sleeping in the house overnight." They also indicate that when they find the right home for them, they will list their house with Sarah.

Sarah explains that it might be difficult to find sellers who will let them "sleep over," so they concentrate on looking at unoccupied properties. They find a house from which the sellers have moved and they make preparations to "sleep over" in sleeping bags on the living room floor. By 3 a.m., Mrs. Byrd is in such great distress that they vacate the property. That contract is terminated! Eventually, after several "sleepovers," the Byrds find an acceptable home.

When they list their current home with Sarah, she insists that they note on the disclosure that "current owners are moving because of sensitivity to air quality." Their buyers do not find anything offensive and purchase the home.

1. If buyers are concerned about mold issues, they
   a. can rely on the sellers to disclose any mold problems.
   b. have no rights in determining mold growth.
   c. are responsible for discovering any problems.
   d. can expect the real estate licensee to assist them in determining mold contamination.

2. Which of the following is most likely to protect a buyer's concerns regarding mold and other environmental concerns?
   a. Caveat emptor
   b. Seller Property Disclosure Statement
   c. Seller providing a home inspector's report
   d. Buyer ordering a home inspection

Student Comments

Please provide your comments regarding the basic principle(s) addressed in this case study, and its relevance to the subject matter generally:

_____
_____
_____
_____

Chapter 4 Review Questions

1. All of the following are required for mold to grow EXCEPT
   a. sunlight.
   b. moisture.
   c. oxygen.
   d. warm temperatures.

2. Why is mold more of a problem today?
   a. Poor construction
   b. Airtight construction
   c. Increased use of products made with formaldehyde
   d. More buyer awareness

3. In a bathroom, which of the following is an excellent food source for molds?
   a. Window glass
   b. Old-fashioned tub
   c. Ceramic floor tiles
   d. Carpeting

4. Molds are a type of
   a. chemical contaminant.
   b. fungus
   c. petroleum-based hazard.
   d. lead-based hazardous material.

5. Which of the following is a health problem associated with mold?
   a. Lung cancer
   b. Impaired neurological development
   c. Aggravated asthma
   d. Osteoporosis

6. The primary method used to prevent mold is
   a. frequent use of humidifiers.
   b. to tightly close up the building.
   c. monthly inspections.
   d. moisture control.

7. Which of the following can be used to kill molds to prevent them from spreading?
   a. Air exchangers
   b. Ultraviolet rays
   c. High Efficiency Particulate Acquisition (HEPA) filters
   d. Air fresheners

8. The most complete type of mold testing probably involves
   a. gathering enough spores to grow a culture.
   b. an x-ray fluorescent device.
   c. analyzing chips of paint.
   d. soil borings.

9. Who should handle mold cleanups?
   a. Home inspector
   b. Seller
   c. Buyer
   d. Mold professionals

10. Which of the following, if any, is an acceptable level of mold in a residential property?
    a. None
    b. 4 pCi/L
    c. Micrograms per deciliter
    d. Above 0.01 fiber/cubic centimeter

chapter five

Asbestos

learning objectives

Upon completing this chapter, you will be able to

- identify what asbestos is and the health hazards it presents to humans.
- discuss probable sources of asbestos exposure.
- describe the difference between friable and nonfriable asbestos.
- explain the reasons why preventing exposure to asbestos is so important.
- list three solutions to an asbestos problem and identify the one most recommended.

Key Terms

ACMs	bulk sampling	friable
air sample testing	chrysotile	mesothelioma
asbestosis	encapsulation	nonfriable

What Is Asbestos?

Asbestos is a naturally occurring mineral fiber whose Greek name means *inextinguishable*. For centuries, asbestos has been prized for its fire-resistant qualities and the flexibility that permits it to be woven into cloth. Its long, narrow fibers are often so minuscule that they can only be seen through a microscope. Not only does asbestos have high tensile strength, but its fibers bind well with other materials, making them even stronger.

Greeks and Romans considered asbestos a "miracle mineral" and used asbestos for lamp wicks and for weaving. One of the more ingenious and amusing uses was by Roman restaurant owners. To clean tables, the restaurant owners simply burned the food off the asbestos tablecloths.

Figure 5.1 | Asbestos Rock

Asbestos is a commercial name used for several forms of fibrous silicate minerals (see Figure 5.1). When found in nature it is in a fibrous rock form. Chrysotile is the most common form, but crocidolite and amosite are two lesser used types. Asbestos is mined primarily in Canada, Africa, Eastern Europe, South America, and the United States.

■ Is Asbestos Harmful to Humans?

Yes. Asbestos has been classified as a carcinogen, a cancer-causing material. However, the effects of exposure do not often appear for decades after exposure. The long latency period between initial exposure to asbestos and the development of cancerous tumors is typically 35 to 40 years. For example, before and during World War II, thousands of shipbuilders worked with asbestos insulation, but asbestos-related diseases did not begin to appear in this group until the mid-1960s.

Early symptoms include shortness of breath, breathing difficulty, persistent cough, and sometimes chest and abdominal pain. Survival rates usually range from 4 to 12 months from initial diagnosis, although some people may live longer. Asbestos has been linked to three of the serious diseases listed next and is highly suspect in the fourth disease:

- **Mesothelioma**—Always associated with asbestos, mesothelioma is a rare cancer of the lining of the chest and abdominal cavity. Unfortunately, cases have occurred after only brief exposure (as little as two weeks) to asbestos as well as in the families of workers exposed to asbestos.
- **Asbestosis**—Asbestosis is a severe disease usually associated with prolonged high exposure to asbestos. It is a scarring of the lung tissue that leads to shortness of breath. In severe cases, the scarring is so great that a person cannot get enough oxygen to walk, let alone to live an active life.
- **Lung cancer**—People exposed to asbestos are five times more likely to develop lung cancer than the general population. This incidence increases by 50 times if the person also smokes cigarettes.
- **Digestive system cancers**—While not scientifically linked, asbestos workers have shown higher incidences of stomach, colon, and rectal cancers compared to the general population.

Figure 5.2 | Chrysotile Asbestos (100x)

Source: National Institutes of Health

Exposure to asbestos fibers does not cause immediate symptoms such as itching and sneezing, and most people exposed to asbestos in daily life do not develop these health problems. Unfortunately, the fibers can lodge in the lungs, remaining there for a long time. The diseases mentioned previously may not appear for 10 to 40 years (latency period).

Moreover, some people who were not directly exposed to asbestos (merely working or living close to an asbestos factory or families of workers) have developed asbestos-related diseases. **There are no "safe" limits of exposure to asbestos.**

How Are People Exposed to Asbestos?

Most exposure occurs through inhalation. Asbestos fibers are often so small that, in comparison, a human hair is 1,200 times larger. Many of the fibers are trapped by mucus in the breathing passageways or in nasal hair and expelled. The smallest ones escape the human body's defense systems and penetrate deep into the lungs. Fibers can also enter the digestive tract via food or smoke in a contaminated area.

Asbestos does not pass through the skin.

Where Has Asbestos Been Used?

Because asbestos is plentiful, readily available, and low in cost, it was used extensively in the building trades between 1920 and 1978 (see Figure 5.3). Thousands of products were developed utilizing its fire resistance, high tensile strength, poor heat and electric conductivity, and chemical-resistant properties.

Outdoors, asbestos was used in exterior roofing shingles, siding, and concrete. Indoors, asbestos was used in floor and ceiling tiles, plasters, insulation for pipes and walls, putties, caulks, paints and cements, and more.

Asbestos was used not only by itself but was combined with many other products. Today, these products are called asbestos-containing material (ACM). Most products made today do not contain asbestos. Those few products that still contain asbestos that could be inhaled are required to be labeled as such.

Where Should Property Owners Look for Asbestos?

The following are some common applications where asbestos might be found in older homes:

- Roofing and siding shingles
- Insulation in houses built between 1930 and 1950
- Textured paint and patching compounds used on wall and ceiling joints; use was banned in 1977
- Artificial ashes and embers sold for use in gas-fired fireplaces

Figure 5.3 | Sprayed Asbestos Insulation

Source: State of South Dakota

- Door gaskets in furnaces, wood stoves, and coal stoves
- Older products such as stove-top pads
- Paper, millboard, or cement sheets on walls and floors around wood-burning stoves
- Resilient floor tiles (vinyl asbestos, asphalt, and rubber), the backing on vinyl sheet flooring, and adhesives used for installing floor tile
- Blankets or tapes on hot water and steam pipes in older houses
- Oil and coal furnaces and door gaskets
- Very old electrical wiring insulation

Are All ACMs the Same?

No, they are not. Asbestos-containing materials (ACMs) are divided into two categories: friable and nonfriable (sheathed and/or noncrumbling).

Friable ACM contains more than one percent asbestos and can be easily crumbled by hand pressure. (Some states monitor materials containing less than one percent asbestos.) Usually, friable ACM is considered the more dangerous of the two types because the particles can be loosened and broken down by the crumbling and become airborne. Once floating freely, they may be inhaled and later cause damage. Examples of friable ACM could include fireproofing on structural beams, sprayed-on asbestos ceiling insulation, and troweled-on acoustical plaster.

Nonfriable ACM can present problems if it is disturbed in any way. Some examples of nonfriable ACM include asbestos cement, asphalt, and vinyl floor tiles. Asbestos is not easily released from these products unless mechanically damaged by rubbing, sanding, cutting, or grinding.

Is Asbestos Easily Recognizable?

No. Products may be suspect because of what they are and where they are used, but the only way to know for sure is by testing. If a possible source of asbestos is found in a home, don't panic. Treat the material as though it were ACM and have it sampled and tested by an expert.

How Is Asbestos Testing Done?

Testing for asbestos is done in two stages. First, testing is done to determine that asbestos is present, and second, the air is tested during and after abatement to make sure that the workers are not unduly exposed and that the site has been adequately cleaned. Most states require certified personnel to do commercial sampling, testing, and cleanup.

- **Bulk sample test**—A certified inspector, after wetting the surface, removes a core sample or scrapes the surface, places the material in a clean, labeled container, and sends it to a qualified lab. In the lab, only an electron or a polarizing light microscope (PLM) can identify both the percentage and the type of asbestos present in the sample.
- **Air sample testing**—The Phase Contrast Microscopic method (PCM) is fast and widely available and requires very little preparation. Unfortunately, this

less expensive test ($20 to $50 per sample) is not specific for asbestos and the smallest fibers are not counted.

If levels above 0.01 fiber/cubic centimeter are found, additional testing by the Transmission Electron Microscopy method (TEM) is required. TEM is slower and more expensive ($100 to $300 per sample), but it is specific for asbestos.

■ Why Is It So Important to Prevent Exposure to Asbestos?

The body cannot break down asbestos fibers trapped in the lungs, and each additional exposure adds a burden to the body. Sadly, asbestos-related diseases are rarely curable, underscoring the need to prevent exposure in the first place.

As long as the fibers remain in the lungs and there is not a way to remove them, a person is at risk for developing a lung disease. One cannot turn back the clock.

■ What Is the Solution When Finding Asbestos in a Building?

If the asbestos material is in good shape and will not be disturbed, do nothing! If this is not possible or not permissible, one of the following three methods may apply:

1. **Encapsulation**—Sealing involves treating the material with a sealant that either binds the asbestos fibers together or coats the material so fibers are not released. Pipe, furnace, and boiler insulation can sometimes be repaired this way. This should be done only by a professional trained to handle asbestos safely.
2. **Enclosure**—Covering exposed insulated piping with a protective wrap or jacket prevents the release of fibers. If the problem is asbestos-insulated pipes in a crawlspace, that area can be sealed off from the main living space. Such entrances should be clearly marked so that future owners are forewarned before entering the area.
3. **Removal**—Asbestos removal is very expensive and, unless required by state or local regulations, should be the last option considered because it poses the greatest risk for fiber release. Removal is complex and should only be done by trained, certified, and insured asbestos professionals.

During removal, the work area should be contained by plastic and put under negative pressure using negative air machines utilizing high-efficiency particulate air (HEPA) filters to help prevent asbestos fibers from traveling out of the work area into other parts of the building. After removal, an independent third party should verify that the asbestos has been removed and that the air is clean.

■ Who Is Permitted to Test for and Remove Asbestos?

Trained asbestos professionals can conduct home inspections, take samples of suspected material, assess its condition, and advise about what corrections are needed and who is qualified to make those corrections. When hiring a professional, the property owner should check credentials carefully and ask for references from previous clients.

To find out whether your state has a training and certification program for asbestos removal contractors and for information on the EPA's asbestos programs, call the EPA at (202) 554-1404. The National Institute for Standards and Technology (NIST) can provide a list of certified laboratories: Laboratory Accreditation Administration, NIST, Gaithersburg, MD 20899 [(301) 975-4016]. Also, call the EPA at (202) 554-1401 for information and a current list of qualified labs to do testing.

■ Are There Laws Regarding Asbestos?

The EPA used the authority it was granted by the Toxic Substance Control Act (TSCA) to ban the production of most asbestos-containing materials (ACM). The federal Asbestos Hazard Emergency Response Act requires certification for any work done with asbestos in schools.

Most states manage the federal EPA regulations outlined in the National Emission Standards for Hazardous Air Pollutants (NESHAP). In 1994, amendments were published outlining regulations regarding the minimum federal qualifications for asbestos workers and their certification requirements. Residential structures with less than four units within the building are exempt from this regulation.

■ Are There Any Safe Substitutes for Asbestos?

There are not really any safe substitutes for asbestos. A few studies done on replacements such as fiberglass and mineral wool seem to indicate that glass fibers and nonasbestos mineral fibers may cause the same kind of lung scarring and cancers that asbestos does. Until more information is available, people should avoid exposure to these products as well as to asbestos.

■ What Should Real Estate Licensees Remember?

Many homes and office buildings may contain ACMs. If asbestos is suspected, licensees and their clients and customers should *not* attempt removal without first testing. Consult your local health department and talk with your state asbestos agency. Remember that in general, encapsulation or containment is usually preferable to attempting to remove asbestos.

Lenders have become extremely careful about buying any property today that may contain asbestos. Commercial and industrial real estate agents must be prepared to supply sources of information to their clients and to negotiate around the presence and removal of asbestos.

Real estate agents should be cautious in offering opinions. Encourage the use of certified testers independent of those doing the abatement.

■ Where Can I Get More Information?

1. The **EPA "Asbestos in Your Home" Web site** is an excellent source of information on asbestos: *http://www.epa.gov/asbestos/ashome.html*
2. The **American Lung Association** offers valuable information about numerous lung diseases, including mesothelioma (asbestos-induced cancer). For infor-

mation go to their Web site: *http://www.lungusa.org*, then click the "Diseases A to Z" tab at the top of the screen, then choose "M" from the screen that appears.

3. The **National Institutes of Health** has more in-depth information on asbestos-related diseases as well as many other environment-related illnesses: *http://ehp.niehs.nih.gov/docs/allpubs.html*

case study

Myron McIntosh is selling his old home in Red Bank, New Jersey, without the help of a real estate broker. Myron has no idea how his home was constructed. However, he is aware that asbestos has been a problem in the area, so he has had his home tested by experts for the presence of asbestos-containing materials. The tests reveal that the basement floor is made of asbestos cement.

Liam and Glenda Wallace are looking for a home with some character that they can remodel. They love Red Bank, and they see some good possibilities in Myron's house. They call Jon Faber, their real estate agent, and ask him to arrange a visit. During the visit, Myron tells them about the asbestos cement. He explains that they don't need to worry—his lawyer told him the floor presents no health problems because it contains nonfriable asbestos. Liam says the terms friable and nonfriable mean the same thing for all practical purposes. Myron responds that even if that is true, the floor is in good shape and obviously will never be moved, therefore posing no danger. The Wallaces agree that the floor is in good shape and won't be disturbed. However, the articles they have read say that any asbestos-containing material should be removed from a home. They turn to Jon for his opinion.

1. Most experts say that if asbestos-containing material found in a building is in good shape and will not be disturbed, the ideal solution is
   a. removal.
   b. enclosure.
   c. encapsulation.
   d. to do nothing.

2. The primary difference between friable and nonfriable asbestos is
   a. friable asbestos usually is sheathed or protected.
   b. nonfriable asbestos can be easily crumbled by hand pressure.
   c. asbestos is not easily released from nonfriable asbestos products.
   d. little or no difference.

Student Comments

Please provide your comments regarding the basic principle(s) addressed in this case study, and its relevance to the subject matter generally:

_____

_____

_____

_____

Chapter 5 Review Questions

1. What is asbestos?
   a. Naturally occurring mineral fiber
   b. Rare, brittle mineral
   c. Man-made extruded fiber
   d. Naturally occurring plant fiber

2. Cigarette smokers should be aware of asbestos issues because they
   a. may develop brown lung disease when exposed to asbestos in small amounts.
   b. and nonsmokers have similar odds of developing asbestos-related cancers.
   c. are less likely to develop asbestos-related cancers than nonsmokers.
   d. are more likely to develop asbestos-related cancer than nonsmokers.

3. How does asbestos become a health hazard?
   a. Only when exposed to water
   b. When it crumbles into tiny, airborne particles
   c. When heated above 360 degrees and the asbestos gas is released
   d. If improperly installed, asbestos continues to emit dangerous fumes

4. If the presence of asbestos is suspected,
   a. the EPA conducts tests for a small fee.
   b. the licensee should recommend that the material be tested.
   c. the material should be encapsulated before testing.
   d. federal law requires that it be tested.

5. Asbestos-related diseases
   a. are rarely curable.
   b. are usually curable.
   c. gradually cure themselves if the asbestos source is removed.
   d. are somewhat contagious.

6. Fiberglass and mineral wool are
   a. secondary forms of asbestos.
   b. used to encapsulate asbestos.
   c. not safe substitutes for asbestos.
   d. safe replacements for asbestos.

7. In the residential real estate transaction, residential real estate licensees should
   a. inspect client homes for asbestos during the walk-through.
   b. not be too knowledgeable about asbestos.
   c. become experts about asbestos.
   d. have a working knowledge about asbestos.

8. If asbestos is found in a home, the first action taken should be to
   a. remove it from the premises as soon as possible.
   b. do nothing if it is in good shape and unlikely to be disturbed.
   c. call the EPA to conduct an inspection.
   d. vacate the property until the problem is solved.

9. The term friable ACM refers to
   a. asbestos-containing material where the asbestos is fully encapsulated.
   b. materials found in nature that contain low levels of asbestos.
   c. a form of asbestos that is easily crumbled.
   d. materials containing less than one percent asbestos.

10. The federal Asbestos Hazard Emergency Response Act
    a. requires certification of work done with asbestos in schools.
    b. authorizes the EPA to condemn residential properties with ACMs.
    c. requires asbestos inspections for homes built prior to 1978.
    d. bans the production of asbestos-containing materials.

chapter six

Volatile Organic Compounds (VOCs) and Pesticides

learning objectives

Upon completing this chapter, you will be able to

- describe formaldehyde and explain its hazard to health.
- identify probable sources of formaldehyde fumes and how a homeowner can avoid them.
- discuss urea formaldehyde foam insulation (UFFI) and explain when it may be a problem to some people.
- discuss pesticides, who uses them, and their health hazards.
- summarize at least four concerns to think about before hiring a pest control company.
- discuss reasons for "sick building syndrome."
- Differentiate between "sick building syndrome" and "building-related illness."

■ Key Terms

building-related illness (BRI)
FIFRA
formaldehyde
pesticides
sick building syndrome (SBS)
toxicity
urea formaldehyde foam insulation (UFFI)
volatile organic compounds (VOCs)

■ What Are VOCs?

At room temperature, volatile organic compounds (VOCs) are emitted as gases from certain solids or liquids. VOCs include a variety of chemicals, some of which may have short-term and long-term effects. One EPA study found indoor levels of VOCs up to ten times higher than those outdoors, even in areas with significant outdoor air pollution sources, such as a petrochemical plant. Examples of VOCs include benzene, methylene chloride (an industrial solvent), trichloroethylene (used in septic system cleaners), and tetrachloroethylene (used in the dry-cleaning industry).

This first section focuses on formaldehyde, one of the most common and problematic VOCs found inside buildings. The second section discusses pesticides. The last section looks at the effects of the concentration of VOCs in buildings.

■ What Is Formaldehyde?

Formaldehyde is a colorless, organic chemical that usually has a pronounced strong odor. It is one of the few indoor air pollutants that can be readily measured. Formaldehyde is an inexpensive preservative (used as an embalming fluid) and bonding agent (used in home insulation and pressed wood products). It was originally considered harmless and so was widely used. It is also a highly flammable liquid/gas and a dangerous fire hazard. About 99 percent of the formaldehyde ends up in the air, the rest in water.

■ Is Formaldehyde a Health Hazard?

The EPA has classified formaldehyde as a "probable human carcinogen" (causing cancer in animals and probably in humans). Many scientists feel that there is no "safe" level of exposure to carcinogens, so avoidance is the best suggestion.

Long-term effects include skin allergies, an asthma-like allergy (shortness of breath, wheezing, chest tightness), and possible bronchitis (coughing, shortness of breath).

■ Is Formaldehyde Poisoning a Concern?

The term *poisoning* is not generally used to describe reactions to formaldehyde. Rather it is a sensitivity or an allergic reaction to the chemical. Often the eyes, nose, and throat are irritated by exposure.

Some estimate that about 10 percent to 20 percent of the population is allergic to or hypersensitive to formaldehyde. Some people develop sensitivity to formaldehyde after intense exposure during a home or office renovation.

Formaldehyde concentrations, duration of exposure, and individual sensitivity affect how intense a reaction may be. It is important to remember that reactions may not be noticed at the time of contact with formaldehyde, but instead, reactions may be delayed for hours.

■ Is Sensitivity to Formaldehyde a Life-Threatening Condition?

Sensitivity to formaldehyde is possibly life-threatening since an extreme reaction could include pulmonary edema (a buildup of fluid in the lungs) and/or a spasm in the windpipe. Both are medical emergencies. More often sensitivity affects the quality of life.

Problems for sensitive individuals can include coughing and sneezing, vomiting and nosebleeds, nose and throat irritation, and headaches and dizziness. Some people are so affected that they have to live away from many man-made products in specially designed homes that are constructed without formaldehyde.

■ Where Is Formaldehyde Found in a Home?

Figure 6.1 | Installing Foam Insulation (UFFI)

Source: Courtesy of NAHB Research Center

Formaldehyde can be found just about everywhere in a home; the possibilities are endless in a typical home. Billions of pounds are produced annually just in the United States, representing up to eight percent of our gross national product.

Formaldehyde-based resins are components of building materials, such as finishes, plywood, paneling, fiberboard, particleboard, subflooring, and paneling, all widely used in manufactured and conventional homes. Formaldehyde is also used in making furniture and cabinets.

Urea formaldehyde foam insulation (UFFI) (see Figure 6.1) helps keep homes warm. Once banned in homes and schools by the Consumer Product Safety Commission, UFFI is once again legal, but rarely used. Generally, UFFI emissions are greatest during the first few months after installation, but vapors may be released if the UFFI is exposed to extreme heat or moisture.

Formaldehyde is used in pesticides, fungicides, and insecticides, and, in solution, as a disinfectant. In manufacturing processes, its uses range from tanning hides to producing explosives.

In homes, many paper products like grocery bags, waxed paper, paper towels, and facial tissues are treated with formaldehyde to increase strength. Formaldehyde increases cleaning power and thus is found in many household cleaning supplies. Floor coverings and permanent press material are often treated by urea formaldehyde as a stiffener, providing both wrinkle resistance and fire retardance.

■ Is Formaldehyde Found in Places Besides Homes and Workplaces?

Formaldehyde is found in many industrial discharges, appearing in rivers and streams and is extremely toxic to animals, birds, and fish. Since formaldehyde may be a result of incomplete combustion of organic matter such as coal and wood, it may be found in the air over industrial areas. Sensitive individuals may choose not to live in such areas.

■ Is There a Formaldehyde Test?

Yes. Trained, qualified professionals can provide more detailed information, but do-it-yourself kits are available to provide a "ballpark" figure of formaldehyde levels. Testing should be done for at least 24 hours to ensure that the sampling period is representative. Heat and humidity tend to increase formaldehyde emissions, so when testing, normal temperature and humidity conditions of the tested site should be replicated.

■ Has the EPA Set Any Standards for "Safe" or "Allowable" Levels?

No "safe" or "allowable" levels have been set in the United States at this time, although countries in Western Europe have set levels, including Sweden, Germany, and the Netherlands. The most widely accepted level is 0.1 part per million (ppm), the limit in the manned space flights and recommended by the American Society of Heating, Refrigeration, and Air Conditioning Engineers (ASHRAE).

■ Is Anything Being Done to Reduce Indoor Air Pollution from Formaldehyde?

Yes, the Consumer Product Safety Commission, the Department of Housing and Urban Development (HUD), and other federal agencies are working with the pressed wood industry to reduce the emission levels of pressed wood.

■ What Can a Homeowner Do to Reduce Exposure to Formaldehyde?

Homeowners who feel they have a serious formaldehyde contamination problem should contact their state authority or regional EPA office for assistance in determining the most appropriate solution.

Purchases of new carpeting, draperies, or furniture should be done in the spring and summer so that windows can be left open as much as possible when the formaldehyde fumes are the greatest. Look for formaldehyde-free or low-emitting furniture and pressed-wood products.

The easiest and least expensive solution is to increase ventilation, often by simply opening opposing windows and doors as frequently as possible. Installing or using exhaust fans may also help.

If the source can be identified, removing it may be best. This works well with paneling, furniture, or carpeting, but may be difficult if the formaldehyde is coming from insulation, particleboard, or subflooring.

Sometimes, the source can be "sealed" with coverings of vapor-barrier paint, vinyl wallpaper, or other special coatings. If the source is insulation, sealing cracks in walls and putting gaskets on electrical outlets may help. Formaldehyde-free varnish, shellac, or special sealers may help in sealing paneling, plywood, or particleboard.

Although expensive and requiring a fair amount of monitoring, chemical air filters can reduce contaminants in the air. Air-to-heat exchange ventilation systems may help by drawing in fresh air while also retaining heat.

■ What Should Real Estate Licensees Be Aware Of?

Agents should check their state's property disclosure form to see if urea formaldehyde foam insulation (UFFI) is a hazard that must be disclosed. Unfortunately, present owners may not be aware of building materials used by previous owners.

Buyers who indicate sensitivity to formaldehyde probably want to avoid newer homes, particularly manufactured homes and mobile homes. Their airtight construction traps fumes emitted by particleboard.

If buyers are contemplating new construction, they should consult early on with the builder to inquire about using products that are low in or free of urea formaldehyde. Owners of older, resale homes may not be aware of formaldehyde products used in construction. Again, remember that the likelihood of emissions after several years is greatly reduced.

■ Where Can I Get More Information?

The following free literature is available:

- For formaldehyde:
  http://www.cpsc.gov/
- "The Inside Story: A Guide to Indoor Air Quality" is a useful brochure available from the EPA's Indoor Air Quality Web site:
  http://www.epa.gov/iaq/pubs/insidest.html
  or call (800) 438-4318.
- U.S. Consumer Product Safety Commission toll-free hot line:
  (800) 638-2772.
  For specific information, go to their Web site and search for formaldehyde:
  http://www.cpsc.gov.

■ What Are Pesticides and Who Uses Them?

Insects, weeds, fungi, rodents, cockroaches, fleas, and termites are everywhere. To get rid of them, chemicals are used, and "-cide" in pesticide means "to kill." Pesticides include plant growth regulators, insecticides, herbicides, fungicides, rodenticides, and disinfectants. Some pesticides are restricted to use only by certified trained specialists, and others are freely available even in grocery stores.

Restricted-use pesticide record-keeping requirements have been adopted on both the federal and state levels. At the very least, for some chemicals, the name of the pesticide, date of application, name of applicator, location, and weather conditions are required to be recorded within 48 hours and the records are to be kept for a minimum of three years.

Unfortunately, up to 80 to 90 percent of most exposures occur indoors, and measurable levels of up to a dozen pesticides have been found in the air inside homes. In fact, studies have shown that the air in our homes and offices may be even more polluted than the outdoor air. Not all of these can be explained by the owner's use of pesticides. Other possible sources of contamination include contaminated soil or dust tracked in from the outside, stored pesticide containers, and household surfaces that collect and then release the pesticide.

■ Are Pesticides a Health Problem?

Definitely. Even limited exposure can cause symptoms that mimic the flu—headache, dizziness, sleepiness, watery eyes, breathing difficulties, muscular weakness, and nausea.

Long-term exposure and/or inadequate treatment may cause allergies, cancer, birth defects, and damage to kidneys, liver, and the respiratory or nervous systems. In fact, the following are so dangerous that their use has been banned: cyclodiene, chlordane, aldrin, dieldrin, and heptachlor (the last may only be used by utility companies to control fire ants in underground cable boxes).

In addition to the active ingredient, pesticides are also made up of "inert" ingredients that are used to carry the active ingredient. Inerts are not toxic to the targeted pest. Unfortunately, some inerts are possible human carcinogens and/or may cause other human health problems.

Several factors are considered regarding injury caused by pesticides:

- **Toxicity**—While some pesticides, such as pyrethrums, have low human toxicity, others like sodium fluoroacetate are extremely deadly.
- **Dose**—The amount of risk is directly related to the dose and the weight of the person. Since children are smaller, they can be poisoned by a lower exposure than an adult.
- **Route of absorption**—Swallowing a pesticide usually causes the most serious problem, but the most common route is through the skin. Some of the most toxic poisons can cause death through skin absorption.
- **Duration of risk**—Usually, the longer one is exposed, the higher the level in the body.

■ Where Are We Exposed to Pesticides and How Can We Prevent Exposure?

To limit exposure, the EPA registers pesticides for use and requires a manufacturer to put information on the label about when and how to use the pesticide. These labels carry the weight of law and, in fact, are the law regarding the use and disposition of the specific container of pesticide to which the label is attached.

Although homeowners are rarely prosecuted for pesticide misuse, they frequently overapply or use the incorrect chemical for a particular pest. Actually, misapplication of lawn care products is the second largest cause of groundwater pollution, just slightly less than that caused by commercial farm herbicide use.

Not all of these are of concern to the real estate agent. For instance, much lifetime contamination is through food, but what people eat is not part of the real estate transaction.

Exposure Through Water

When pesticides are applied to land, a certain amount may run off into streams and rivers. If applied to sandy soil over a groundwater source, pesticides may leach through the soil to the groundwater. Today, agricultural pesticide use is regulated, reducing contamination, but a lot of contamination is a result of inappropriate or excessive use by residential property owners.

The EPA's water program sets standards and provides advisory levels for pesticides and other chemicals which may be found in the drinking water. Public municipal water systems are regularly tested, but private wells usually are not unless the owner specifically requests testing. It is recommended that well water used for drinking should be tested as part of the transaction. In fact, such testing may be required in some areas.

Exposure Through the Air

Air currents may carry pesticides that were applied to the property next door or one that is several miles away. Some properties are located next to fields regularly receiving pesticide treatment and thus are vulnerable to receiving exposure.

Planting trees as a buffer zone may cut down on the pollution coming from the spraying of adjacent fields. Some communities have enacted "right-to-know" ordinances which require public notification when spraying is being done.

Exposure Inside the Home

Finally, it is very possible that pesticides have been heavily used inside a home and have settled on surfaces. In that case, all surfaces, including cracks and crevices, have to be thoroughly scrubbed. In some situations, soap and water is not enough. In that case, consult a knowledgeable professional for appropriate cleaning materials.

Are There Federal Guidelines?

The Federal Insecticide, Fungicide, and Rodenticide Act (FIFRA) governs the registration of pesticides and prohibits the use of any pesticide product in a manner that is inconsistent with the product labeling. Still, thousands of pesticide products are available for use in and around homes. Unfortunately, there are no federal guidelines for indoor air quality.

Where Do Pesticides Fit Into the Real Estate Transaction?

Obviously, farm brokers should be aware of state regulations regarding agricultural field spraying for they may be asked to supply additional information to buyers. They should be aware of any "right-to-know" laws that would affect new buyers.

In residential sales, licensees are often asked to recommend pest control services. Licensees should avoid recommending a particular company but can caution buyers to look carefully at several companies before making a decision. Here are some points to consider when evaluating a company:

- Does the company offer natural and/or petrochemical-free insecticides or alternative treatments?
- Is the company affiliated with a professional pest control association that helps educate its members with new safety and training as well as requiring them to abide by a code of ethics?

- Will the company work closely with the buyer when considering specific concerns regarding allergies, age of occupants (very young or very old), or pets (especially fish aquariums)?
- Can the company produce documentation that the company is insured, including insurance for sudden and accidental pollution?
- Does the Better Business Bureau have any complaints about the company on file?

What Is "Sick Building Syndrome"?

The World Health Organization estimates that up to 30 percent of new or remodeled commercial buildings have unusually high rates of health and comfort complaints of headaches, fatigue and sleepiness, irritation to eyes and nose, dry throat, general loss of concentration, and nausea. Studies monitoring indoor air quality indicate a complex mix of pollutants, any one of which can cause problems: formaldehyde, radon, carbon monoxide, sulfur dioxide, ozone, molds, and particulates such as tobacco smoke, dust, and pollen.

A main problem is using space in a building for which it was not originally designed, especially with inadequate amounts of outdoor "makeup" air. Also suspect are the presence of pollution from pesticides applied by pest management practices and formaldehyde from pressed wood, particularly in new or recently remodeled buildings. Other factors may be involved, such as fluorescent lighting, air that is too hot or dry, a buildup of positive ions, and a lack of individual control of the environment.

These environmental problems contribute to the "sick building syndrome." Owners and managers of office buildings and residential rentals are often called upon to deal with these elusive, but quite real, issues.

Generally, the term "sick building" has been applied only to commercial properties and public buildings such as hotels, offices, and so on. Following are the guidelines used by the EPA to identify building-related illnesses.

- **Sick building syndrome (SBS)**—The EPA considers people to be suffering from "Sick Building Syndrome" when at least 20 percent of the occupants complain of a particular discomfort, and the discomfort is alleviated upon leaving the building. In addition, no link to the source of discomfort has been found.
- **Building-related illness (BRI)**—The EPA considers sickness to be a "building-related illness" only when there is an identifiable personal injury with a direct link to a known causative agent. An example might be Legionnaires' disease, where the cause is a known bacterium sometimes found in air conditioner cooling towers that gets into the ventilation ductwork. When inhaled, the bacterium causes serious respiratory illness, and even death.

Where Can I Get More Information?

- **The EPA** Web site has much more information on pesticides as well as links to other sites and publications: *http://www.epa.gov/iaq/pesticid.html*

- **National Pesticide Telecommunications Network:**
  It has two useful booklets, with single copies available for a mailing fee of $2: "Healthy Lawn, Healthy Environment" and "Citizen's Guide to Pesticides." (800) 858-7378
  http://ace.orst.edu/info/nptn/
- Both booklets are also available from the **National Center for Environmental Publications and Information (NCEPI):** (800) 490-9198
  http://www.epa.gov/ncepihom/catalog/
- Other useful booklets include:
  "Indoor Air Pollution: An Introduction for Health Professionals"
  "The Inside Story: A Guide to Indoor Air Quality"
  "Introduction to Indoor Air Quality: A Self-Paced Learning Module"
  "Introduction to Indoor Air Quality: A Reference Manual"
- **Indoor Air Quality Information Clearinghouse,** a service of the U.S. EPA: (800) 438-4318

case study

Lily and Thomas Terrapin are planning to buy their first home and they contact a real estate agent for assistance. They have a one-year-old daughter so they are concerned about lead-based paint hazards. Also, Lily has had difficulties with rashes and breathing and at least one doctor has suggested that she is extremely sensitive or allergic to formaldehyde, so finding a home without formaldehyde is Lily's primary concern. Her agent, Nancy Glick, is surprised to hear about this allergy, saying, "Well, I am not sure how we can deal with this." Thomas wants to know how to find a good pest control company since they don't want to have any insects in their new home.

Nancy gets on the Internet and starts her research. She learns that formaldehyde is present just about everywhere, and she copies some of the information to share with Lily. She learns that most modern building materials are treated with formaldehyde in order to increase strength and fire retardance.

1. Which of the following can Nancy suggest to the Terrapins?
   a. Concentrate on newer homes, particularly manufactured and modular homes
   b. Explain that most homes on the market meet the EPA standard for "safe" levels of formaldehyde
   c. Look at older homes and test for lead
   d. Suggest that Lily see another specialist to get another medical opinion

2. Nancy can most effectively help Thomas handle potential pesticide problems by
   a. helping him evaluate providers of pest control services.
   b. suggesting that he interview several pest control companies.
   c. giving him a list of the federal guidelines for indoor air quality.
   d. asking the sellers if they ever used pesticides inside the home.

Student Comments

Please provide your comments regarding the basic principle(s) addressed in this case study, and its relevance to the subject matter generally:

_____

_____

_____

_____

Chapter 6 Review Questions

1. Formaldehyde is generally found in
   a. newer construction.
   b. older factories.
   c. homes built before 1978.
   d. office buildings with excellent ventilation.

2. One striking characteristic of formaldehyde is that it
   a. is colorless and odorless.
   b. takes a long time to break down.
   c. has a strong, pronounced odor.
   d. rarely is a problem to anyone.

3. What standards meet the EPA "safe" levels for formaldehyde?
   a. Up to 4 parts are allowable
   b. 10 to 20 parts
   c. Differs whether in an office building or residential dwelling
   d. No safe or allowable levels

4. All of the following building materials may have been manufactured with formaldehyde EXCEPT
   a. UFFI.
   b. solid oak tongue and groove wood floors.
   c. fiberboard walls and plywood subflooring.
   d. newly installed carpeting.

5. An office building property manager is planning to upgrade all of the carpeting and drapes in the building. When is the best time to schedule the renovation?
   a. At the time most convenient to the tenants who will have to vacate the building for seven to ten days
   b. Any time during the year as long as enough notice is given to the tenants
   c. Fall and winter
   d. Spring and summer

6. What is the meaning of "-cide" found at the end of some names of environmental concerns?
   a. A guarantee that the product is okay for human use
   b. To kill an organism
   c. Restricts the product to outdoor use only, not indoor
   d. Product is safe for animal exposure but not exposure to humans

7. Which of the following is the second most common source of groundwater pollution?
   a. Misapplication of lawn care products
   b. Excessive commercial farm herbicide use
   c. Emission leaks from older factories
   d. Gasoline by-products such as lead

8. The most frequent cause of problems from pesticides is due to
   a. passing from one person to another by sneezing and coughing.
   b. inhalation.
   c. absorption through the skin.
   d. ingestion.

9. What is the intent of the Federal Insecticide, Fungicide, and Rodenticide Act (FIFRA)?
   a. To determine acceptable standards for pesticide usage
   b. To govern the registration of pesticides and to prohibit using products inconsistent with the labeling
   c. To mandate testing and to regulate laboratories
   d. To inspect factories and commercial farming operations for incorrect pesticide usage

10. Which of the following can contribute to "sick building syndrome"?
    a. Lead-based paint
    b. Asbestos
    c. Formaldehyde
    d. Chlorine

chapter seven

Drinking Water

learning objectives

Upon completing this chapter, you will be able to

- summarize the importance of clean water.
- list at least five water contaminants and the health hazard of each.
- name the two most common methods of removing contaminants from water.
- emphasize that private wells are most at risk for contamination and discuss testing before any real estate transfer.

■ Key Terms

| chlorine | cryptosporidium | nitrates |
| coliform bacteria | giardia | Safe Drinking Water Act |

■ What Is the Importance of Safe Drinking Water?

The human body is approximately 66 percent water. We can live for nearly a month with no food, but less than a week without water. Water is the single most important essential element we can ingest. There are varying opinions on how much water we should drink, but nearly all agree that we need between four to eight glasses of water a day. Water assists in the digestion and absorption of food, in maintaining proper muscle tone, ridding the body of wastes, and helping to serve as a natural air conditioning system. Surprisingly, water even helps brain function. Even moderate dehydration can affect our mental abilities.

The surface of the earth is about 70 percent water, although only about one percent of that water is drinkable. By the time water reaches our faucets, it has passed through inorganic and organic matter, chemicals, and other contaminants. As a natural solvent, it may leach a bit of everything it has passed through.

Americans tend to expect their tap water to be safe, and it is generally more safe than in most countries. Unfortunately, many cities have water treatment systems predating

World War II, and these are proving inadequate today. As a result, many individuals are boiling their water or buying bottled water. Since there are no federal standards for bottled water, there is also no guarantee that it is any purer than tap water.

■ What Are the Most Common Water Contaminants and Their Health Effects?

Water, in the form of rain, cleanses the air of airborne pollutants. Rainwater is then further compromised by surface pollutants, so by the time it washes into rivers, lakes, and aquifers, it carries with it many of the chemicals generated by man. Some of the most common contaminants include the following:

- **Nitrates**—Manure and fertilizers, containing high levels of phosphorus and nitrogen, may leach into water supplies. Some studies have linked nitrate contamination to stomach and liver cancer as well as to reproductive problems.

- **Lead**—The primary source of lead in water is a result of water being carried through pipes that contain lead or lead solder and water coming in contact with brass faucets (brass is about 8 percent lead). Unfortunately, even if the water leaves the public water treatment plant free of lead, there is no guarantee that it will arrive in the home as pure.

    Even if lead is present in very low levels in the water supply, accumulations can build up in the body over time to unsafe levels and become a health threat, detailed in Chapter 2. Such effects are often irreversible, particularly in small children.

- **Radon**—Compared to radon entering the home through soil, entrance through water is a very small source. However, radon present in the water supply can be released through showerheads into the air or through other household uses of water. Radon is more of a concern in private wells than in public water supplies.

    Radon can be removed from the water before it enters the house. As mentioned in Chapter 3, long-term exposure to radon may lead to an increased probability of lung cancer, particularly if coupled with tobacco smoking.

- **VOCs**—The EPA estimates that VOCs (benzene, industrial solvents, dry-cleaning solvents, etc.) are present in nearly 20 percent of the nation's water supplies. Spilled on the ground surface, VOCs are absorbed by the soil and may eventually reach the water source. The EPA has established maximum contaminant levels (MCL) for each chemical, many of which produce a sweet, pleasant odor in water.

    At the very least, VOCs irritate the skin and the mucous membranes when inhaled. Higher levels of exposure result in drowsiness and even stupor. Since little is known about the additive effects of these chemicals, it is recommended that water should not be drunk if it contains two or more contaminants. Whenever possible, identifying and preventing further contamination is the safest solution. Gasoline products should not be used near the source of underground or surface water.

- **Pesticides**—Fungicides, insecticides, and herbicides, after doing their job of killing pests, soak into the ground. However, most agricultural chemicals are registered and monitored. Private homeowners use tremendous amounts of pesticides, possibly incorrectly, and these too eventually find their way into our water supplies. As discussed in Chapter 5, pesticides may cause flulike symptoms, and some are possible human carcinogens.

Table 7.1 | When to Test Your Water

Conditions or Nearby Activities	Recommended Test
Recurrent gastrointestinal illness	coliform bacteria
Household plumbing contains lead	pH, lead, copper
Radon in indoor air or region is radon-rich	radon
Scaly residues, soaps don't lather	hardness
Water softener needed to treat hardness	manganese, iron (before purchase)
Stained plumbing fixtures, laundry	iron, copper, manganese
Objectionable taste or smell	hydrogen sulphide, corrosion, metals
Water appears cloudy, frothy, or colored	color, detergents
Corrosion of pipes, plumbing	corrosion, pH, lead
Rapid wear of water treatment equipment	pH, corrosion
Nearby areas of intensive agriculture	nitrate, pesticides, coliform bacteria
Coal or other mining operation nearby	metals, pH, corrosion
Gas drilling operation nearby	chloride, sodium, barium, strontium
Odor of gasoline or oil, near gas station or buried fuel tanks	volatile organic compounds
Dump, junkyard, factory, or dry-cleaning operation nearby	VOCs, TDS, pH, sulfate, chloride, metals
Salty taste, seawater, or heavily salted roadway nearby	chloride, TDS, sodium

- **Chlorine**—An inexpensive and easy-to-produce corrosive, poisonous, greenish-yellow gas, chlorine is first liquefied and then mixed into drinking water and swimming pools to destroy all animal and microbial life (bacteria).

  Long thought to be harmless, today there is evidence that chlorine may combine with organic compounds, and it is possible that these chlorination by-products are harmful. In epidemiological studies, increased bladder and rectal cancer risks appear to be associated with excessive exposure to chlorination by-products. Although few suggest that chlorination be eliminated, alternatives to chlorination for the disinfecting of drinking water are being explored.

- **Giardia and Cryptosporidium**—These microscopic parasites (see Figure 7.1) are commonly found in lakes and rivers when contaminated by sewage and animal waste. They may be found in up to 97 percent of the surface water supplies and nearly two-fifths of drinking water supplies. Giardia is the most frequent cause for diarrhea in North America.

  To eliminate the problem, the cysts require long exposure to chlorine disinfection or submicron filtration. Unfortunately, many cities and small rural communities do not have the latest filtration devices, and most probably, private well owners do not.

  Once ingested, the cysts cause cholera-like illnesses with symptoms of watery diarrhea, headache, abdominal cramps, nausea, and low-grade fevers. Severe damage can occur in the liver and respiratory tract in the very young, the very old, and anyone with suppressed immune systems. Outbreaks have occurred even in communities served by municipal water systems (Milwaukee, Wisconsin 1993, and Las Vegas, Nevada 1994).

Figure 7.1 | Giardia Lamblia

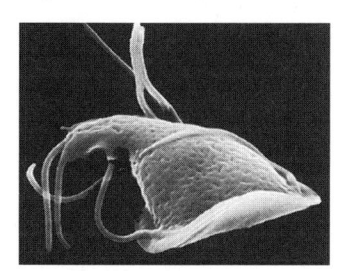

Source: National Park Service

What Is the Solution?

The best solution is source protection and regular testing, followed by chlorination and filtration. With the growing awareness of the importance of preventing contamination in the first place, many municipalities are designating watershed areas to protect their water supply. Watersheds are better protected and more carefully monitored than other areas. Often there are specific guidelines for actions to be taken in the event of a spill or other pollution source.

Certainly, private well owners should seek to prevent spills of gasoline, pesticides, and so on, anywhere near their water source. Any well located near an industrial site or in close proximity to underground storage tank water should be tested for volatile organic compounds (VOCs).

When Should Water Be Tested?

Water should be tested routinely once a year for nitrates, pH, total dissolved solids (TDS), and coliform bacteria (found in animal and human waste). Testing should be done during the spring or summer after a rainy period to provide a "typical" sampling of the water. These tests should also be done after repairing or replacing an old well or pipes, and after installing a new well or pump. Buyers can include a testing contingency clause in their offers to purchase.

Testing for sulfate, chloride, iron, manganese, hardness, and corrosion index should be done every three years. If the home plumbing contains lead materials, brass fittings, or lead solder, the water should be tested as soon as possible whether on municipal or private well water. (The use of lead in new or replacement plumbing materials has been banned by Congress.)

Sometimes, special situations develop that indicate a need to test the well water. For instance, if the taste, odor, or color of water changes, or someone has recurring gastrointestinal problems, it may be time to test. If a baby is expected in the household, testing for nitrates should be done early in the pregnancy, before bringing the infant home, and again six months later.

Where Can Water Be Tested?

Private testing laboratories are listed in the telephone book and on the Internet. A state health department lab certification officer can verify that they are certified. The Safe Drinking Water Hotline at (800) 426-4791 can provide the number of the nearest certification officer. Local engineering firms, county and state health laboratories, departments of health, and local hospital and university laboratories may also provide testing resources. Sometimes water treatment companies and plumbing supply stores may offer certain tests in the home for free.

A record of all water test results should be kept as reference for future testing. Comparison of original and recent test results assists in determining whether a change in treatment is needed or that a treatment device is not working as it should. Also, these records are valuable when transferring property and making proper seller disclosures.

■ Are There Federal Laws to Protect Our Water Supplies?

Yes, there are federal laws regulating water supplies, beginning with the federal Safe Drinking Water Act (SWDA) created in 1974 to protect public health. Subsequent amendments proved extremely difficult and expensive to implement. In 1996, the act was amended to make it simpler for water treatment facilities to comply with federal regulations.

In its present form, SWDA requires each state to submit an annual report on public water system violations to the EPA. The report must address violations of national primary drinking water regulations with respect to maximum contaminant levels (MCLs), treatment techniques, significant monitoring requirements, and variances and exemptions. States must publish and distribute summaries of their reports to the public.

The 1996 SDWA Amendments were further strengthened in 2000. The EPA published revised regulations that require water suppliers to report any situation that poses a health risk within 24 hours, instead of the previous 72 hours. Additionally, water suppliers can combine reports to reduce the number overall and to make those notices easier to understand. Systems serving less than 10,000 people may be eligible for an exemption, even though these systems may be older and more suspect. If the first quarterly series does not detect certain contaminants, repeat testing may not be required. Grant money is available to assist and encourage small water treatment systems to comply.

In summary, this legislation gives states greater flexibility in identifying contamination in potable water supplies, more consumer information in an easy-to-understand format, and greater attention to assessing and protecting sources of drinking water. New minimum standards are being established for certification and recertification for water system operators.

■ How Does This Affect the Real Estate Licensee?

Many seller property disclosure forms require sellers to indicate water source, such as municipal water supply, well water, or other. When anything other than municipal is indicated, agents should ask sellers about well-water testing, and suggest that those reports be made part of the property disclosure.

Buyer agents should certainly suggest to buyers that they have well water analyzed before closing to determine water quality, especially if the property is a current or former agricultural or industrial site or buried fuel tanks are located nearby. If contaminants are found, options include preventing further contamination, locating an alternative water supply, or treating the water to remove the contaminants. Buyers should remember that the time to negotiate is before, not after, settlement.

If sellers indicate that they have been using a home filter system, buyers should ask why and what kind. Systems may be at each faucet (point-of-use) or where water enters the home (point-of-entry). The most effective are reverse osmosis and filters removing particles smaller than one micrometer in diameter. Bacteria can live on carbon filter surfaces so they must be cleaned frequently.

Where Can I Get More Information?

- **EPA Ground Water and Drinking Water Web site**:
  The EPA site is an excellent source of information regarding all aspects of groundwater and drinking water.
  http://www.epa.gov/ogwdw/index.html
- **Certified Testing Services:** For information on certified testing services in your state:
  http://www.epa.gov/safewater/privatewells/labs.html
- **Local Cooperative Extension Offices and Health Departments** may also provide lists of certified private laboratories to do water testing. If you are unable to find a local testing service, the following EPA Web site provides you with contact information for the office in your state that certifies water testing laboratories:
  http://www.epa.gov/safewater/faq/sco.html
- **The Safe Drinking Water Hotline**:
  For specific questions about local drinking water and/or various types of water treatment systems.
  hotline: sdwa@epa.gov
  (800) 426-4791

case study

A young couple with two small children found a "fixer upper" property for sale on a wooded lot in the area where they wanted to live. The property was adjacent to an abandoned old gas station, but it was screened by trees and shrubbery, so its presence didn't diminish their interest in the home. The husband was a real handyman and felt confident he could tackle the repairs and renovations the home needed, so they called the office number listed on the For Sale sign.

The licensee on duty told the couple he would be pleased to show them the property that afternoon. In preparation for the showing, the agent pulled the listing information from the office computer, which showed that the in-house listing was priced at $89,500, and had been on the market for more than nine months. The agent also noted that it was a three-bedroom, 1,700 square feet home, built in 1979, and apparently had never been connected to city water and sewer.

1. At the first meeting with the potential buyers, the licensee should
   a. suggest to the buyers that they should have the well tested.
   b. tell the buyers to ask the sellers to test the well as this might help the home sell more quickly.
   c. offer no suggestions about testing the well to the potential buyers.
   d. provide the buyers with the company's "Tips for Buying a Home" pamphlet and let them make their own decision regarding testing.

2. What, if anything, should the licensee say about the adjoining abandoned gas station?
   a. Nothing; the buyers are capable of making their own decisions
   b. Encourage the buyer to contact the local health department for guidance
   c. Point out the gas station and then remain quiet
   d. Suggest that the buyers consider soil testing for possible gas contamination

Student Comments

Please provide your comments regarding the basic principle(s) addressed in this case study, and its relevance to the subject matter generally:

_____

_____

_____

_____

Chapter 7 Review Questions

1. Without water, humans can generally live
   a. less than 3 days.
   b. longer than they can without food.
   c. less than one week.
   d. 8 to 10 days.

2. Regarding purity, rainwater
   a. is cleaner than most municipal water.
   b. cleanses the air as it falls.
   c. is purified by chlorine in the atmosphere.
   d. is as clean as distilled water.

3. The main sources of nitrate contamination in drinking water are
   a. dumps and toxic waste sites.
   b. manure and fertilizers.
   c. acid rain from coal burning power plants.
   d. deteriorated plumbing systems.

4. When should well water be tested?
   a. During or shortly after a rainy spell
   b. In dry summer months
   c. During all residential property transfers
   d. Only upon request by the buyer

5. What is cryptosporidium?
   a. Type of mold
   b. Sexually transmitted disease
   c. Dissolved mineral
   d. Microscopic parasite

6. What is the **best** solution for maintaining pure water?
   a. Source protection
   b. Liberal use of chlorine
   c. Regular testing
   d. Filtration

7. What are watersheds?
   a. Federally protected wetlands
   b. Buildings used for hydroponic farming
   c. Tanks used to hold rainwater runoffs from large paved areas
   d. Areas where water runoff enters or affects water supplies

8. How safe is bottled water?
   a. Safer than municipal water
   b. Must meet EPA standards
   c. Less safe than municipal water
   d. Is not required to meet federal testing standards

9. When, if ever, is water testing required?
   a. For all FHA closings
   b. By most seller property disclosure forms
   c. For rural properties only
   d. Rarely required, but well water should be regularly tested

10. Changes made in 1996 to the Safe Drinking Water Act
    a. made it easier for water treatment systems to comply with federal regulations.
    b. require states to submit all water test results to the EPA.
    c. added provisions for testing bottled water.
    d. raised the allowable level of arsenic in municipal water supplies.

chapter eight

Other Indoor Pollutants

learning objectives

Upon completing this chapter, you will be able to

- define biological pollutants and list the two conditions for biological growth.
- list three ways to prevent or eliminate biological pollutants.
- summarize what buyers and tenants should look for before moving in.
- define combustion pollutants and explain how they are harmful to health.
- name the primary combustion pollutant and describe health symptoms as a result of this environmental hazard.
- list the steps to take if confronted by possible carbon monoxide poisoning.
- list at least three toxic substances used in and/or released during methamphetamine production.
- describe the procedures used to mitigate buildings contaminated by meth pollutants.

■ Key Terms

| biological pollutants | combustion pollutants | methamphetamine |
| carbon monoxide | environmental tobacco smoke (ETS) | meth lab |

■ What Are Other Sources of Indoor Air Pollution?

Most homes and businesses have more than one source of indoor air pollution. Indoor air quality may be compromised by inadequate ventilation, overcrowding, and the presence of pollutants such as environmental tobacco smoke (ETS), biologicals, such as molds, excessive formaldehyde, and organic gases released from household cleaning products, air fresheners, and so on. In fact, the EPA notes that indoor air pollutants in homes can be up to 10 to 200 times worse than the outdoor ambient air. This chapter looks at biological pollutants other than mold (discussed in Chapter 4) as well as combustion pollutants, and contains a

73

section on meth labs due to the rise in methamphetamine use and its clandestine manufacture, often in homes.

■ What Are Biological Pollutants?

Biological pollutants are or were living organisms that promote poor indoor air quality. Often invisible, they can travel through the air, causing poor health and even damage to surfaces in and outside the house. Some of the more common ones are animal dander, dust mites and cockroach parts, fungi (molds), infectious agents (bacteria or viruses), and pollen.

Infectious diseases caused by bacteria and viruses can be easily spread in crowded conditions with poor air circulation, common to modern design and architecture. Conditions necessary for biological growth, nutrition, and moisture can be found in many homes: bathrooms, damp basements, wet appliances, and even some carpets and furniture. Allergic reactions can range from mildly uncomfortable to life-threatening, such as an asthma attack.

■ What Are the Health Issues?

Some well-defined illnesses, such as Legionnaires' disease, hypersensitivity pneumonitis, and humidifier fever, can be directly related to specific building problems and are called building-related illnesses (BRIs). Some of these diseases are quite serious, resulting in death, while others are treatable.

However, others are less well-defined, and the following symptoms may indicate poor indoor air quality: dryness or burning in the nose, eyes, and throat; sneezing; stuffy or runny nose; fatigue or lethargy; headache; dizziness; nausea; irritability; and forgetfulness. Sick Building Syndrome (SBS) is when these symptoms are present, and no specific cause can be determined. See Chapter 6 for more information on SBS.

One major health issue is asthma, especially in children. Today, nearly one-third of asthma cases involve children under the age of five. Some research suggests that deteriorating indoor air quality may be responsible for the increase in asthma cases worldwide, especially in industrialized countries like the United States. In addition to pollutants previously mentioned, indoor air quality is compromised by the presence of cockroaches, house dust mites, and dander from pets.

■ What Can Be Done to Prevent or Eliminate Biological Pollutants?

Newer, tightly sealed homes have significantly increased the number of indoor air quality problems found in homes and other buildings (see Construction Issues, Chapter 11). Steps must be taken to prevent or reduce buildups. The EPA recommends three basic strategies:

- Source control
- Ventilation improvements
- Air cleaners

Owners and landlords should try to control moisture in the building. This includes fixing leaks and seepage, installing and using exhaust fans, cleaning rugs and carpeting more often, ventilating crawlspaces, and placing plastic covers over dirt to prevent moisture from coming indoors.

Also, all appliances that come in contact with water, such as furnaces, heat pumps, central air conditioners, dehumidifiers, and humidifiers, should be maintained and kept as clean as possible. Owners should replace moldy shower curtains and clean all surfaces thoroughly. Painting over without first cleaning is usually not sufficient as the mold can resurface.

Probably the most effective action property owners can take to improve the overall air quality in their homes is to install air exchangers and HEPA filters (High Efficiency Particulate Air Filters). Air exchangers are an energy-efficient addition to heating and air conditioning systems that allow cleaner outdoor air to replace stale indoor air on a continuous basis (see Chapter 11 for more information). HEPA filters can be used with the air exchangers to trap very small dust, mites, pollens, and so on.

What Is the Role of Real Estate Licensees?

Agents can encourage buyers and tenants to thoroughly inspect their new homes before closing or moving in. Early inspection can leave time for negotiating corrections. The following is a helpful checklist for identifying those problems:

- Have professionals check the heating and cooling systems, including humidifiers, vents, duct lining, and insulation, looking for mold growth.
- Check exhaust fans in the kitchen and bathrooms. If these are not vented, is there at least one window in the kitchen and bath?
- Go through the house, including the attic, basement, and crawlspaces, looking for obvious mold growth. Also, check to see that the downspouts route water away from the house.
- Note any, and if possible, remove rotten materials and stains on ceilings, floors, and carpeting that may indicate leaks or moisture problems.
- Ask if the previous owners or tenants owned pets. If so, fleas, mites, dander, or urea odors may be a problem.
- Look for signs of cockroaches.

Where Can I Get More Information?

- Your local **American Lung Association** can provide several pamphlets, including "Indoor Air Pollution Fact Sheets" and "Air Pollution in Your Home?"
- Contact the **U.S. Consumer Product Safety Commission**, Washington, DC 20207 for "The Inside Story: A Guide to Indoor Air Quality," "Biological Pollutants in Your Home," and "Humidifier Safety Alert."
- **Indoor Air Quality Clearinghouse**
  P.O. Box 37133, Washington, DC 20013-7133
  (800) 438-4318
  "Flood Cleanup: Avoiding Indoor Air Quality Problems."

- The **EPA Indoor Air Quality Division's Carbon Monoxide** Web site has more information and numerous links to sites on the topic:
  http://www.epa.gov/iaq/co.html
- For issues relating to the workplace, consult **The Occupational and Safety Health Administration (OSHA)** Web site
  http://www.osha.gov/SLTC/indoorairquality/recognition.html

What Are Combustion Pollutants?

Combustion pollutants are primarily gases or particles that come from burning materials and include carbon monoxide, nitrogen dioxide, sulfur dioxide, and ash particulates. Although faulty venting in office buildings and other nonresidential structures has resulted in combustion product problems, most cases involve the home.

Combustion pollutants come from vented or unvented appliances, space heaters, gas ranges and ovens that are malfunctioning, gas furnaces, improperly vented fireplaces, water heaters and clothes dryers, wood or coal burning stoves, and improperly used kerosene or gas space heaters.

Environmental Tobacco Smoke (ETS)

The effects of ETS may become an issue when owners put a house on the market. Tobacco smoke lingers not only in the air, but also as residue in the carpeting, woodwork, and walls, producing a stain that may be nearly impossible to remove. Sellers should be forewarned that prospective buyers may make lower offers to offset the expense of removing the residue or may decline to make any offer at all.

What Is Carbon Monoxide?

Carbon monoxide, often referred to as CO (its chemical name), is a colorless, odorless, tasteless gas released in small amounts during normal combustion. However, the amount of CO released increases dramatically when there is incomplete combustion due to a lack of sufficient oxygen.

Average levels in homes without gas stoves vary from 0.5 to 5 parts per million (ppm). Levels near properly adjusted gas stoves are often 5 to 15 ppm, and those near poorly adjusted stoves may be 30 ppm or higher.

What Health Problems Have Been Noted?

Health problems from combustion pollutants range from headaches, breathing problems, and increased risk of respiratory infections to death. Some contaminants are carcinogenic. Combustion produces water vapor which can encourage the growth of biological pollutants mentioned earlier and also may result in structural damage.

However, the much more common problem is carbon monoxide buildup. Red blood cells in our body pick up carbon monoxide more readily than oxygen. At higher concentrations of CO in the air, the body replaces increasing amounts of oxygen with CO, which leads to tissue damage.

At low concentrations, healthy people become drowsy. People with heart disease may experience chest pain. Symptoms at higher concentrations include impaired vision and coordination, headaches, dizziness, confusion, and nausea. Sometimes excessive carbon monoxide exposure causes flulike symptoms that clear up after leaving home. At very high concentrations, carbon monoxide poisoning is fatal.

■ What Are Acceptable Indoor Levels of CO?

No standards for CO have been agreed upon for indoor air. The U.S. National Ambient Air Quality Standards for outdoor air are 9 ppm (40,000 micrograms per meter cubic) for 8 hours, and 35 ppm for 1 hour.

■ How Does Carbon Monoxide Build Up to Fatal Levels?

Improperly adjusted gas ranges and unvented gas or kerosene heaters contribute to high concentrations of CO in indoor air. Worn or poorly adjusted boilers or furnaces can also be significant sources, especially if the flue is improperly sized, blocked, disconnected, or is leaking. Auto, truck, or bus exhaust from attached garages, nearby roads, or parking areas can also be a source. Unfortunately, many carbon monoxide fatalities are a result of people cooking indoors with charcoal-fired hibachis or barbeques or using these devices for supplemental heating.

■ How Is Carbon Monoxide Poisoning Treated?

Treating carbon monoxide poisoning requires getting oxygen back into the person's blood system as fast as possible. Anyone confronted with a situation where CO poisoning appears to be involved should do the following:

- **Evacuate**—Move the affected person to fresh air. Administer oxygen if available.
- **Contact medical help**—If the person is not breathing, perform artificial respiration as taught in cardiopulmonary resuscitation training until medical help arrives.
- **Ventilate**—Ventilate the area by opening doors and windows and turning on ventilation fans (heater and air-conditioning fan for example).
- **Investigate**—If possible, after the building is ventilated, find the source of the problem and turn it off until it is repaired.

■ What Can Landlords and Homeowners Do to Reduce Combustion Pollutants?

The most important step is to use combustion appliances correctly and make sure they are properly vented. Using only vented appliances, as opposed to unvented devices, is also helpful. Installing carbon monoxide detectors is another important step.

Owners should follow the recommendations of the manufacturer. In general, the flame of the furnace combustion chamber should be checked at the beginning of the heating season (usually in the fall) to see that the flame burns mostly blue (not yellow), and flues and chimneys should be inspected and cleaned at least once a year.

When installing a woodstove, make sure to choose the properly sized unit for the space being heated, and that it meets EPA emission standards. When using it, make certain the doors fit tightly and all gaskets are in good condition.

■ Where Does the Real Estate Licensee Fit In?

Property managers should be sure that the heating appliances are properly installed and scheduled for regular maintenance. Regular use of space heaters should be avoided. Agents for buyers and tenants should suggest independent inspections of heating and air-conditioning units before closing or moving in. Agents should encourage sellers to fully disclose the working condition of all combustion devices.

Unless all appliances and heating systems are electric, the property should be equipped with carbon monoxide detectors. These should be placed in the areas where the nonelectric devices are located, i.e., the kitchen for a gas range, near the furnace and/or water heater, in the vicinity of a woodstove, and so on.

■ Have There Been Any Lawsuits?

Yes! Apart from the big settlements, licensees should be aware that carbon monoxide injures and kills! In 2001, more than $30 million was paid to seven former tenants of Terra Cotta Apartments near Miami Lakes. The plaintiffs alleged that a broken water heater spewed the noxious gas, causing blackouts and brain damage. One woman died a day after moving into the apartment at the complex, which had previously been closed by the Department of Health. Her teenage daughter and two friends were comatose for days.

In February 2000, the parents of two children who died in their sleep of carbon monoxide poisoning were awarded $1.7 million in a wrongful death lawsuit in St. Cloud, MN. Apparently, a previous home inspection report indicated a faulty furnace, but the Stearns County family was not informed. The jury found the real estate licensees and their companies 65 percent responsible and the previous owners 35 percent. (*Burt v Neubarth et al*, C3-96-2506)

> **A TRUE STORY**
>
> In Vermont, a seller (who was also a real estate licensee) did not reveal to the buyer that the gas-fired boiler in his basement had a lethal defect even after being warned by a plumbing company repairman. Later, three people died from carbon monoxide poisoning. This was the first time in Vermont that the state's real estate disclosure law had been used in a manslaughter case. The seller is now incarcerated with a four-year prison sentence and faces additional civil action.

■ Where Can I Get More Information?

- Check out the **EPA** Web site for tips on buying woodstoves and a list of EPA-certified stoves:
  http://www.epa.gov/compliance/monitoring/programs/woodstoves/

- For safety information on kerosene heaters and other combustion-based appliances go to the **Consumer Product Safety Commission** Web site and search for the type of product (kerosene, gas range, etc.): *http://www.cpsc.gov/cpscpub/pubs/pub_idx.html*
- The following Web site is a good source of general information on carbon monoxide: *http://www.carbonmonoxidekills.com/*
- For information on carbon monoxide detectors check out: *http://www.codetection.com/*

■ What Are Meth Labs and Where Are They Found?

Meth labs are the places where methamphetamines are manufactured (see Figure 8.1). Meth "labs" can be housed in all types of buildings and enclosures ranging from RVs to motels and apartments to upscale residential houses. They can be found throughout the United States and are located in cities, suburbs, rural areas, and remote locations. The desire for secrecy has made the large lightly populated rural Midwest an especially attractive venue for meth production.

The chemicals used to make meth and the by-products from the process are highly toxic. The desire for secrecy and lax practices used by meth makers ("cooks") often leave the buildings and grounds surrounding them more contaminated than many federally designated toxic waste sites. This is becoming an increasing problem in the transfer of residential real estate.

■ What Are Methamphetamines?

Methamphetamines include a range of addictive, mood-altering drugs used increasingly throughout the United States and the world. There are many forms including "crank," "crystal-meth," "glass," and "ice," among others. They may be smoked, snorted, ingested, or injected depending on the type. They produce an intense pleasurable "rush" in users that can last from minutes to hours. Meth has a rapid tolerance buildup, so that more must be used each time to obtain the same "high." Meth, especially ecstasy, has become the drug of choice for many and has led to a dramatic increase in illicit drug use since the early 1990s.

Figure 8.1 | Meth Lab

Source: Criminal Intelligence Service Alberta

■ What Are the Problems Associated with Meth and Meth Labs?

The many medical problems associated with meth use are beyond the scope of this text. However, from an environmental and real estate point of view, serious issues are generally related in some way to illegal methamphetamine operations or "meth labs."

Unfortunately, methamphetamines are relatively easy to make, requiring easily obtainable but extremely dangerous materials. Some of them are highly flammable or toxic VOCs, including acetone, methanol, and chlorofluoroethane (CFE). Others are severely corrosive, caustic, or poisonous including anhydrous ammonia (a farm chemical), sodium hydroxide (lye), ethylene glycol (antifreeze), and sulfuric acid (drain cleaner). The process can also involve the use of toxic metals such as lithium (from batteries) and phosphorus (extracted from garden chemicals).

Meth Labs Costly for Unsuspecting Property Owners

In May 2004, the Associated Press ran a story about the discovery and cleanup of a Clinton, Tennessee methamphetamine lab in a $500 per month mobile home rental. The report said that after authorities got rid of the chemicals and cooking stoves from the meth lab, the cost of decontaminating the home fell to the property owner, and that the home could not be rerented until cleanup was complete.

The owner said he had paid in excess of $25,000 to clean up the property, and he still didn't know what needed to be done before he could relet the property.

In other cases, the AP said, property clean-up costs have exceeded $70,000 with no way for owners to recover money. Very few jurisdictions require disclosures for future owners or tenants of the homes, so owners and real estate licensees face a rapidly increasing potential for serious legal problems.

The facilities and surroundings used for meth production and waste disposal can be more dangerous than EPA-registered toxic waste sites. According to the Office of National Drug Policy, production of one pound of methamphetamine can release between five to seven pounds of toxic waste while releasing poisonous gases into the atmosphere.

Chemical fumes released during manufacture can accumulate on work surfaces, in walls, furniture, carpeting, drapes, and heating and air-conditioning ducts. Toxic wastes from the process are often flushed down sinks and toilets. Places used to store the ingredients may be contaminated from leaks or spills. The wastes dumped outside might seep into underground water supplies and run over to adjacent properties, contaminating those properties as well.

■ How are Meth Labs Cleaned Up?

In some areas of the country, many officials simply burn the property to the ground, although this may be more symbolic than a necessary action. Only professionals using protective equipment and methods associated with other toxic waste sites should EVER attempt any cleanup.

Essentially, the process involves any or all of the following:

- **Removal**—All furnishings, including carpeting, paneling, wallpaper, and any other furnishings that cannot be adequately cleaned are removed.

- **Ventilation**—The building must be extensively ventilated to remove any solvents or other chemical fumes that may have been built up.
- **Neutralization**—Any remaining residue must be neutralized either by detergent-washing, steam-cleaning, or high-pressure cleaning. This means that all walls, floors, ceilings, counter surfaces, and so on must be thoroughly cleaned.
- **Encapsulation**—If cleaning is not possible, sometimes the contamination may be encapsulated or sealed with an oil-based paint, polyurethane, or other material.

■ What Is the Impact on Real Estate Transactions?

In 2003, government-paid contractors cleaned up more than 7,700 meth-contaminated properties nationwide. Tennessee led the nation with nearly 1,100 sites. These are only a small portion of the properties involved. In some municipalities the sheriff and or city police have the properties burned to the ground.

Properties suspected or identified as meth lab sites should not be rented, sold, or otherwise reoccupied until verification is provided showing that they have been evaluated and cleaned by certified professionals. Disclosure to buyers is critical, and should include special warnings if the buyers have or are likely to have children.

Figure 8.2 | Seller's Disclosure of Information on the Production of Methamphetamines

---

SELLER'S DISCLOSURE OF INFORMATION ON THE PRODUCTION OF METHAMPHETAMINES

Pursuant to South Dakota Codified Law, in any selling of a residential premise, any seller who has actual knowledge of the existence of any prior manufacturing of methamphetamines on the premises shall disclose that information to any purchaser or any person who may become a purchaser.

Seller's Disclosure (initial)

_____(a) Presence of existence of any prior manufacturing of methamphetamines (check one below):

☐ Seller has knowledge of the existence of any prior manufacturing of methamphetamines on the property (explain).
_____
_____

☐ Seller has no knowledge of the existence of any prior manufacturing of methamphetamines on the property (explain).

Certification of Accuracy
The following parties have reviewed the information above and certify to the best of their knowledge, that the information provided by the signatory is true and accurate.

_____ _____ _____ _____
Seller   Date   Buyer   Date

_____ _____ _____ _____
Seller   Date   Buyer   Date

Source: South Dakota Real Estate Commission

Adjacent properties may be stigmatized or contaminated by their proximity to the former lab. Because of the health issues involved, many feel that licensees should disclose the issue.

However, sometimes, real estate licensees and property managers are the ones who make a discovery from such telltale signs as the following:

- covered or blackened windows and being denied access to the property
- sweet, ammonia, or solvent-like chemical smells
- an accumulation of propane cylinders and/or antifreeze containers
- Pyrex or other glass containers with tubing duct-taped to them
- red-stained coffee filters or linens (used to filter red phosphorus)

For both health and safety reasons, an individual who believes he or she has discovered an illegal drug lab should immediately leave the premises and notify local law enforcement.

case study

The Speicher family is negotiating with Ron and Celia Tamori from upstate New York to sell the Speicher farm in Elizabethtown, Kentucky. The Speichers have declared that the main farmhouse is free of any problems and that all of the appliances, even the space heaters in the upstairs bedrooms, are in good working order.

The agent for the Tamoris, Terry Labronski, explains to the Tamoris that the Speichers' declaration means there are no problems with biological or combustion pollutants. To reassure the Tamoris, Terry has conducted a personal inspection of the basement floor and walls and personally checked all of the space heaters. He says his inspections confirm the Speichers' declaration.

Shortly after the purchase, the Tamoris move into the house. Celia Tamori experiences frequent headaches and feels nauseous much of the time. One morning her daughter is unconscious and is hospitalized with what is diagnosed as carbon monoxide poisoning. The neighbors also inform Mr. Tamori that the Speichers had complained of poor health, and they had wondered "if something is wrong with the house." Public health officials later discovered that the space heaters in the upstairs bedrooms were improperly burning and thus intermittently producing carbon monoxide.

1. How should a real estate licensee respond when discussing the seller disclosure to the buyers?
   a. Just as this agent did; tell the buyers to trust the seller disclosure and then back it up with his own inspection
   b. Encourage the buyers to obtain their own home inspection
   c. Inform the buyers to talk with the neighbors about any problems the sellers may have hidden
   d. Tell the buyers to buy a new furnace and new space heaters, as a matter of course

2. What was the "red flag" that should have alerted the real estate licensee to potential problems?
   a. None; there was nothing out of the ordinary
   b. Farmhouse considered "old"
   c. Sellers declare "no problems"
   d. Routine use of space heaters

Student Comments

Please provide your comments regarding the basic principle(s) addressed in this case study, and its relevance to the subject matter generally:

_____
_____
_____
_____

Chapter 8 Review Questions

1. What are combustion pollutants?
   a. Inert gases produced by lead smelting plants
   b. By-products of industrial manufacturing
   c. Naturally occurring gases
   d. Gases or particles that result from burning materials

2. Health symptoms posed by combustion pollutants include
   a. increased lung cancer potential, especially for cigarette smokers.
   b. skin rashes and asthma symptoms.
   c. headaches, drowsiness, and confusion.
   d. damage to growing neurological systems, such as brain development and motor skills.

3. At what time of the year should owners schedule furnace inspections?
   a. Spring
   b. Summer
   c. Fall
   d. Winter

4. How often should chimney flues be inspected?
   a. Every six months
   b. Once a year
   c. Every other year
   d. Whenever the property is sold

5. In which of the following situations could the owner consider NOT installing a carbon monoxide detector?
   a. All electric house
   b. All gas house
   c. Home with supplemental heat supplied by a wood-burning stove
   d. Home with supplemental heat supplied by kerosene space heaters

6. The house is heated by an electric heat pump located outside, cooking is done on a gas stove in the kitchen, and electric space heaters supplement the heat pump in the upstairs bedrooms. Where, if anywhere, should the carbon monoxide detector be placed?
   a. In the kitchen next to the stove
   b. In the basement
   c. In each of the upstairs bedrooms where the electric space heaters are located
   d. Not anywhere since there is no potential for carbon monoxide

7. If a licensee walks into a home and finds unconscious people and suspects carbon monoxide as the cause, what is the first thing that the licensee should do?
   a. Pull the people out into fresh air
   b. Open the windows
   c. Call for help
   d. Start CPR

8. All of the following can contribute to serious health problems, but which one can cause death in a matter of just a few hours?
   a. Lead poisoning
   b. Asbestos
   c. Carbon monoxide
   d. Radon

9. Property owners who want to improve indoor air quality should do all of the following EXCEPT
   a. control the source.
   b. improve ventilation.
   c. install air fresheners.
   d. install air cleaners.

10. A real estate licensee arrives to show a property. There are several empty containers of antifreeze and a sweet smell in the air. Inside, the licensee can see red-colored coffee filters on the dining room table. What toxic hazard should the licensee suspect?
    a. Lead-based paint
    b. Asbestos
    c. Carbon monoxide
    d. Methamphetamines

part C

Outdoor Environmental Issues

chapter nine

Underground Storage Tanks

learning objectives

Upon completing this chapter, you will be able to

- describe the federal government's definition of an underground storage tank (UST).
- list three ways to test for leaking underground storage tanks.
- explain why the EPA has decided to let states monitor USTs.
- name the date by which all tanks must have spill, overflow, and corrosion protection.
- list at least three types of tanks that are exempt from compliance.

Key Terms

LUST Trust	soil vapor test	UST
soil borings test	tank integrity test	

What Is an Underground Storage Tank (UST)?

The EPA defines a UST as a tank and any underground piping connected to the tank that has 10 percent or more of its volume beneath the surface of the ground. Prior to the mid–1980s, most USTs were made of bare steel, which is likely to corrode, permitting the stored petroleum or hazardous materials to seep into the soil. Over one million USTs in the United States contain petroleum or hazardous wastes regulated by the U.S. EPA. Many have leaked or are leaking. These releases can cause fires or explosions.

However, a more common and more serious problem is contamination of underground aquifers, i.e., the groundwater sources for drinking water. While it is expensive to clean contaminated soils, it can be catastrophic to decontaminate an aquifer.

Where Are USTs Found?

USTs are found everywhere, not just in industrial areas. In many parts of the country, fuel oil for home heating is kept in underground tanks. Historically, when a tank filled up with groundwater or started to leak, it was replaced. By use of metal detectors and utility locators, multiple tanks have sometimes been located even on residential properties.

What Are the Most Common Testing Methods for Leaking Tanks?

There are three common testing methods:

1. **Soil borings**—This is most often recommended by environmental professionals for a real estate transaction. A decontaminated hand auger is lowered to the bottom of several holes drilled near the UST. A sample is then removed and packed in dry ice and shipped with the proper chain of custody paperwork to an EPA-approved lab. Check with your own state for which method of analysis is preferred.
2. **Tank integrity test**—This is used for the semiannual testing of gas station tanks and is not recommended for a real estate transaction because inaccurate readings may result due to the temperature, air pressure, groundwater fluctuations, and operator error. Based on just one tank integrity test, an owner should not decide on remedial action and a buyer should not make a purchasing decision.
3. **Soil vapor**—After several small shallow holes are drilled near the UST, a probe is inserted. An air sample is pulled through the probe and analyzed for petroleum content. This may not be as effective to discover heating oil tanks since heating oil is not as volatile as gasoline.

How Are Leaking USTs (LUSTs) Cleaned Up?

First, the tank is removed under the supervision of a county authority or fire marshal, cleaned, and properly disposed of. The exposed soil in the hole is inspected to see if it is stained by oil. If so, that soil is removed. Soil will continue to be removed until testing shows no more contamination. Contaminated soil is stockpiled under plastic sheeting or placed in drums and shipped to a hazardous waste landfill or treated with oil-eating bacteria. If the petroleum has leaked to an aquifer or other water source, the state may test wells in the surrounding area to determine the extent of the contamination.

All newly installed USTs must have a number of safety features, including double wall construction with the outer wall being constructed of either corrosion-resistant metal or noncorroding synthetic materials like fiberglass or composites. If the outer wall is metallic, it must be coated with a suitable dielectric material and equipped with a cathodic protection system (these prevent leaching of the metals from the tank by galvanic corrosion). The tank must be installed with overflow and spill prevention systems, as well as leak detection monitors (see Figure 9.1).

What Laws Cover USTs?

Figure 9.1 | Double-walled UST

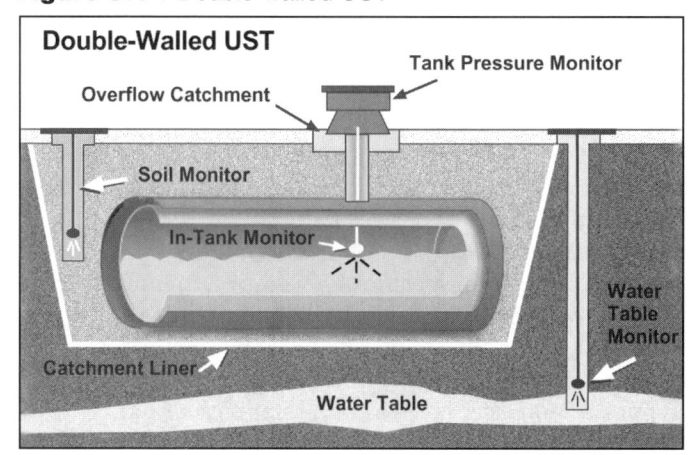

The primary goal of UST regulation is to protect groundwater. A section of the Re-source Conservation and Recovery Act (RCRA) re-quired the EPA to develop a comprehensive regulatory program for USTs storing petroleum or hazardous materials. In 1984, the Hazardous and Solid Waste Amendments Act required owners to find leaks and clean them up.

The Superfund Amendments and Reauthorization Act (SARA) created the Leaking Underground Storage Tanks (LUST) Trust Fund to oversee cleanups by responsible parties and to pay for cleanups at sites where the owner is unknown, unwilling, or unable to respond. It also requires owners to demonstrate financial responsibility for cleaning up releases and spills and to compensate third parties for damages caused by leaking USTs. The LUST trust is funded by a 0.1 cent tax on each gallon of motor fuel sold in the country. By April 1995, about $1.44 billion had been collected.

Because of the enormity and diversity of the UST problem, the EPA has decided that state and local governments are in a better position to oversee USTs. Consequently, one of the provisions of RCRA permits state programs approved by the EPA to operate in lieu of the federal program, resulting in some state requirements that are stricter than federal ones.

States have access to LUST trust fund money when they enter into a cooperative agreement with the EPA. States have allocated and spent about a third of their money on administration, a third for oversight and state lead enforcement activities, and a third for cleanups.

Who Is Affected by These Regulations?

The regulations require owners and operators of USTs to prevent releases, detect releases, and correct the problems created by the releases. Essentially, for a UST installed after December 22, 1988, these owners and operators must prove that they are able to pay for damages caused by toxic spills or releases. Coverage requirements are either $500,000 or $1 million "per occurrence," and either $1 million or $2 million in "aggregate" coverage depending on the operator's ownership category. Failure to meet these requirements may result in citations and fines.

The BIG date was December 1998, when all tanks, even those installed prior to 1988, had to have spill, overflow, and corrosion protection.

Although leaks from the following tanks could contaminate a water supply, at the present time, they are not covered by these regulations:

- Farm and residential tanks holding less than 1,100 gallons of motor fuel used for noncommercial purposes
- Tanks storing heating oil used on the premises where it is stored

- Tanks on or above the floor in basements or tunnels
- Septic tanks and systems for collecting stormwater and wastewater
- Flow-through process tanks
- Tanks containing less than 110 gallons
- Emergency spill and overfill tanks

Anyone interested in USTs should contact their local UST program for specific requirements. Some states have financial assistance programs to provide funds or low-interest loans to help owners upgrade or replace their tanks.

It is important to note that the federal laws specifically exempt farm and residential tanks, although each state has the right to define what a UST is and what needs to be done if there is a spill. Generally, in most states, if petroleum leaks into the environment in detectable amounts, the leak must be reported properly. Failure to report can result in fines or nonacceptance into the state trust fund.

How Common Are USTs?

The American Petroleum Institute estimates that more than ten million homes with underground storage tanks are storing more than eight billion gallons of home heating fuel. They also estimate that there are more than 200,000 abandoned gas stations throughout the U.S. The United States Geological Society estimates that 96 percent of all UST sites contain some form of petroleum product.

The EPA reports that as of the end of January 2004, 1.5 million old, unsafe tanks have closed; almost 300,000 petroleum leaks have been cleaned up; nearly all underground tanks have been upgraded or replaced. In addition, newly discovered leaks have dropped dramatically, from a high of over 66,000 in 1990 to roughly 12,000 in 2003.

How Do USTs Affect Real Estate Licensees?

Disclosure of USTs must, of course, be made to prospective purchasers and lenders. The presence or absence of USTs greatly affects the value and marketability of commercial and industrial sites. It is important in all real estate transactions to look for tanks currently in use as well as abandoned ones.

Real estate licensees are advised to learn more about their own individual state requirements, particularly those related to residential tanks.

Where Can I Get More Information?

The EPA is the best single source of information on USTs. Your state Department of Environmental Quality (DEQ) is another source for local information.

- The EPA's main UST Web site is: *http://www.epa.gov/swerust1/*
- The EPA provides a summary (PDF format) of regulations covering USTs: *http://www.epa.gov/swerust1/pubs/musts.pdf*

- State DEQ Web sites can usually be accessed by entering your two-letter state abbreviation in the following link (Note – replace XX with your state abbreviation): *http://deq.state.XX.us*

case study

Kumar Joshi is a new real estate licensee who is working with his first buyers, Anna and Jacob Gunterman. The Guntermans are ready to purchase a property, but the home inspector thinks that the areas in the back where the grass isn't growing could possibly indicate an underground storage tank. Kumar recently attended a seminar on underground storage tanks (USTs), but he never thought that he would encounter a situation since he is specializing in residential, single-family dwellings.

However, Kumar recommends that the Guntermans hire a consultant to come out and do more testing. Sure enough, the tests show that there probably are tanks in the ground, and faced with this information, the seller says, "Yes, my parents used to store their heating oil in these tanks."

After consulting with the state Department of Environmental Quality, the seller learned that the state offered some financial assistance for removing the tanks, and so the tanks were removed. The Guntermans were pleased that they had spent the extra money on the tests, because now they know that the source of the soil contamination had been removed.

1. When should buyers raise the issue of testing and UST removal?
    a. As part of the buyers' original offer
    b. When the home inspection indicates a problem
    c. After closing
    d. Only if they have a problem in a couple of years after closing

2. Heating oil tanks are most likely going to be part of a
    a. residential real estate transaction.
    b. transfer of 100 acres of pasture and grazing lands.
    c. transfer of a shopping mall.
    d. vacant lot zoned for manufacturing.

Student Comments

Please provide your comments regarding the basic principle(s) addressed in this case study, and its relevance to the subject matter generally:

_____
_____
_____
_____

Chapter 9 Review Questions

1. A storage tank is considered a UST if it
   a. contains toxic substances.
   b. is listed on the EPA National Priority List.
   c. has at least 90 percent of its volume beneath the surface of the ground.
   d. has at least 10 percent or more of its volume beneath the surface of the ground.

2. Residential underground fuel tanks are
   a. exempt from federal regulation.
   b. covered by federal regulation if the property is multifamily units.
   c. exempt from federal regulation if they contain oil, but not if they contain propane.
   d. covered by federal regulation if they contain oil, but not if they contain propane.

3. Regarding steel underground storage tanks, they
   a. are the safest since they rarely leak.
   b. are likely to leak due to corrosion.
   c. will be replaced by stronger tanks made of titanium.
   d. will be replaced by 2006.

4. In most real estate transactions, soil borings are
   a. the best tests to use to determine leaking tanks.
   b. conducted by the U.S. Geological Society.
   c. only used when USTs are known to be leaking.
   d. invalid under EPA guidelines.

5. Where does the LUST Trust obtain its cleanup funds?
   a. Tax on chemical companies
   b. Motor fuel tax
   c. Superfund
   d. Impact fee on new UST installations

6. Under what situations do the states have access to LUST trust fund money?
   a. For new tank installations
   b. To enact new stringent UST laws
   c. For UST monitoring, administering, and clean-up
   d. For environmental use as the state determines

7. By 1998, owners of existing USTs had to
   a. replace any that were made of metal.
   b. install spill, overflow, and corrosion protection.
   c. remove them and install double-walled tanks.
   d. have them EPA-certified.

8. Are USTs still an environmental hazard?
   a. No, since fewer than one million homes still have USTs for home heating fuel storage.
   b. Yes, definitely, since there are more than two million abandoned gas stations in the United States.
   c. No, because the EPA has cleaned up more than 70 percent of all leaking USTs.
   d. Yes, more than 96 percent of USTs contain some form of petroleum product.

9. What is required of newly installed USTs?
   a. Be constructed of fiberglass
   b. Have leak containment systems and leak monitoring devices
   c. Be removable for inspections for leaks every five years
   d. Built with vents to release flammable gas buildup inside the tank

10. What is the effect of USTs in a real estate transaction?
    a. USTs are considered material facts and must be disclosed.
    b. All USTs must be removed before closing.
    c. Only leaking USTs must be removed before closing.
    d. USTs are considered personal property and are not part of the real estate transfer.

chapter ten

Waste Sites and Toxic Substances

learning objectives

Upon completing this chapter, you will be able to

- name and discuss three environmental protection laws concerning toxic substances.
- identify the characteristics of brownfields and what has been done to relieve the issues surrounding them.
- explain the EPA's Hazard Ranking System (HRS), including the factors used to assign them and what they are used for.
- explain the purpose of the Toxic Substances Control Act.
- name three hazardous substances on the EPA Chemical Substance Inventory and explain where they are commonly used and the health risks they pose.

■ Key Terms

Brownfield Act	HRS	SARA
CERCLA	MBTEs	Superfund
CFCs	NPL	TCEs
Hazard Rank System	PCBs	TSCA

■ What Does CERCLA Mean?

Enacted by Congress in late 1980, the Comprehensive Environmental Response, Compensation, and Liability Act (CERCLA) is commonly referred to as the Superfund Act. This law created a tax on chemical and petroleum companies, and gave the federal government broad authority to respond directly to actual or threatened releases of hazardous substances that might endanger public health or the environment.

CERCLA was originally created as a temporary emergency measure to clean up extremely hazardous waste sites such as Love Canal, Times Beach, and others. A majority of these sites were created by unregulated toxic waste dumping from the 1940s until the 1970s when environmental issues became part of the national consciousness. Key provisions of the act were that it:

- gave the EPA authority to identify hazardous sites to be included on the National Priorities List (NPL) for cleanup;
- provided for liability of those responsible for releases of hazardous waste at the identified sites;
- created a trust fund to be used for cleanup when no responsible party could be identified;
- authorized short-term cleanup actions when the hazardous situation required immediate response;
- authorized long-term actions to permanently reduce hazardous conditions at sites that were not immediately life-threatening.

Taxes collected in the first five years of the act created a $1.6 billion trust fund for cleaning up abandoned or uncontrolled hazardous waste sites (thus the name Superfund). By the fall of 2003, a total of 2,129 sites were included on the National Priority List. Cleanup or stabilization has been completed at 886 of them (about 42 percent). The rate of new additions to the list has declined steadily since 1988.

What Is SARA?

The Superfund Amendments and Reauthorization Act (SARA) renewed and amended CERCLA. SARA was enacted in October 1986, and reflects the EPA's experience in managing the Superfund program. The act also included the following changes and additions to CERCLA:

- Stressed the importance of long-term remedies and use of advanced treatment technologies in cleaning up hazardous waste sites;
- Required Superfund actions to consider the standards and regulations found in other state and federal environmental programs;
- Gave the EPA new enforcement authorities and negotiating tools;
- Increased state involvement in every phase of the Superfund program;
- Increased the focus on human health problems posed by hazardous waste sites;
- Encouraged greater citizen input regarding decisions on how sites should be cleaned up;
- Increased the size of the Superfund to $8.5 billion.

What Is the Hazard Ranking System (HRS)?

SARA also required the U.S. EPA to revise the Hazard Ranking System (HRS) to provide a systematic method of evaluating waste sites for placement on the National Priorities List (NPL). HRS is a numeric ranking system based on initial waste site surveys to determine the likelihood that a site may harm people or the environment. It considers the following criteria to assign HRS values:

- likelihood that the site is releasing or could release hazardous substances into the environment;
- type, toxicity, and amount of waste involved;
- people or sensitive environments at risk, i.e. groundwater, surface water, soil, or air.

Because the HRS scores are based only on initial studies, they do not set funding priorities or determine the order in which sites are worked on.

What Is TSCA?

The Toxic Substances Control Act (TSCA), enacted in 1976, gave the EPA the authority to track more than 75,000 known industrial chemicals currently produced or imported into the United States. The EPA repeatedly screens these chemicals and requires reporting or testing of those that may pose an environmental or human health hazard. To date, more than 800 chemicals are listed as toxic. The EPA can ban or restrict the manufacture and import of toxic substances that pose an unreasonable risk.

The EPA also tracks the thousands of new chemicals that industry develops each year with either unknown or dangerous characteristics. The EPA then can control these chemicals as necessary to protect human health and the environment.

What Is the TSCA Chemical Substance Inventory?

The EPA classifies chemical substances as either existing chemicals or new chemicals. Known substances are ones that are listed in the EPA's Chemical Substance Inventory. Any substance that is not on the inventory is classified as a new chemical. Importers and manufacturers must consult this inventory before they can use the substance or bring it into the country.

A new substance can be used for a commercial purpose only if it is subject to an exemption or a TSCA reporting exclusion (for example, a low volume exemption,

Figure 10.1 | Toxic Site

Source: U.S. Environmental Protection Agency

or exclusion as a naturally occurring material). The inventory can be used to determine if there are restrictions on manufacture or use of existing substances.

■ What Are Some of the Banned or Restricted Chemicals?

Most of the 75,000 substances on the TSCA inventory list are not hazardous. They are used for many different purposes or in products we use on a regular basis. On the other hand, others are quite hazardous, and their use is banned or restricted, or under study to see if they should be. Some of the better known items in these categories include:

- **CFCs**—Chlorofluorocarbons are commonly used in air conditioners and refrigerators, solvents, paints, and foam blowing applications. The chlorine-containing CFC vapors eventually rise to the upper atmosphere where they are broken down by ultraviolet light into chemicals that deplete the earth's protective ozone layer. They are being replaced by HFCs, similar chemicals that do not contain chlorine or bromine.

    Consumers should consider upgrading to newer, more environmentally friendly appliances. More importantly, the appliances containing the CFCs must be properly disposed of. The EPA suggests utilizing local CFC-HCFC recovery programs. Only EPA-certified technicians who have passed the EPA-approved exam should be hired to do any work on a refrigeration system. Both the Air Conditioning and Refrigeration Institute (ARI) and the Underwriters Laboratories (UL) are approved by the EPA to offer these certifications.

- **PCBs**—Polychlorinated biphenyls are used in many products including adhesives, paints, carbonless copy paper, and fluorescent light fixtures. PCBs are one of the most widely studied environmental contaminants and are proven carcinogens (cancer-causing) in animals and likely so in humans. They also have other serious health effects affecting the immune system, reproductive system, nervous system, endocrine system, and others.

    In the late 1960s, however, the discovery of PCBs in birds in Sweden and the poisoning of 1,200 Japanese by rice oil containing PCBs got the public's attention, resulting in a halt of production in 1977. Today in the United States, PCBs are found only in existing closed electrical and hydraulic systems. These are being replaced by other equipment as they wear out, but we still hear occasional news stories of PCB spills from old railroad transformers, and so on.

- **MTBE**—Methyl tertiary butyl ether (MTBE) is used as a gasoline additive to improve combustion and thereby reduce air pollution. It has been shown to cause cancer in animals at high doses, but human studies are still in process.

    The larger problem with MTBE is that unlike other petroleum hydrocarbons, it is highly soluble in water and not easily absorbed by soil, and it resists biodegradation. Its widespread, long-term use has the potential to develop high concentrations in groundwater aquifers used for drinking water. Being soluble, it can travel great distances from where it started, thus making it a regional problem that is difficult to trace to its source. Ethanol made from corn is a viable replacement being pushed by many midwestern states.

- **TCE**—Trichloroethylene is a nonflammable, colorless liquid with a somewhat sweet odor and a sweet, burning taste. It is used primarily as a solvent for cleaning metal parts and in the dry cleaning business. It can be found in the home in some spot removers, paint strippers, and typewriter correction fluids. It is a health risk that can potentially affect the nervous system, liver, and kidneys. The EPA classifies it as "highly likely to produce cancer in humans."

Trichloroethylene is not thought to occur naturally in the environment. However, it has been found in underground water sources and many surface waters as a result of the manufacture, use, and disposal of the chemical. It has been found in at least 852 of the 1,430 National Priorities List sites identified by the EPA.

What Are Brownfields?

Brownfields are areas near hazardous waste sites that are economically depressed and may be stigmatized by a real or perceived contamination caused by the waste site. Potential purchasers worry about liability questions. "How clean is clean?" is the issue surrounding abandoned or underutilized urban commercial and industrial sites.

When the EPA first issued regulations for cleanup, it favored treatment or permanent remedies rather than containment. To ensure that some party associated with the problem could be held accountable, the EPA extended liability to include individuals, estates, parent corporations, and lenders. In older, urban areas, these enforcement policies made many industrial sites unmarketable because:

- Lenders did not want to end up with unknown environmental liabilities.
- Landowners avoided voluntary site investigations for fear of mandatory cleanups.
- Rural land, perceived to be more likely free of environmental problems, became very attractive to manufacturing and commercial ventures.

What Is Being Done to Relieve Brownfields?

In 2002, President Bush signed the Small Business Liability Relief and Revitalization Act (the Brownfields Law) that clarifies CERCLA liability provisions for certain landowners and potential property owners. Some states have also begun a more flexible approach aimed at brownfield issues, including flexible cleanup standards, lender liability protection, and financial incentives to persuade developers to consider brownfield sites for redevelopment.

The federal Brownfields Law enables certain contaminated industrial or commercial properties to become economically viable. It allows prospective purchasers and their lenders relief from liability for past contamination that they did not cause. To qualify, the parties involved must meet the following criteria:

- demonstrate that they did not cause, contribute to, or consent to the hazardous condition,
- may not be affiliated with the liable party in any way (familial, financial, contractual),
- must take reasonable steps to stop any release, and prevent or limit human or environmental exposure to the hazardous substances.

The act also provides, at EPA discretion, mechanisms to resolve liability concerns of residential property owners immediately adjacent to a hazardous site.

How Do These Substances Impact Real Estate?

First, real estate licensees are consumers too, so everyone should use products that are environmentally safe. However, licensees face additional duties depending on their real estate specialties and the laws and rules of the state in which they conduct their real estate transactions. As mentioned in the first chapter, licensees should become knowledgeable about environmental issues and recommend that their clients and customers seek expert advice at every step of the transaction.

Moreover, the presence of these substances can substantially impact the value of the property. Not only appraisers but also listing agents working with sellers and agents who represent buyers must be aware of the impact of environmental issues on value and liability. We normally think of these issues as having a negative effect, i.e., loss of property value, increased liability, and so on. However, the 2002 Brownfields Act may make some previously unsaleable properties attractive to commercial buyers.

Specifically, property managers must be aware of not only indoor air quality issues, but must also become knowledgeable about refrigeration and CFCs and their proper disposal. Commercial brokers should advise their clients to do more soil testing for PCBs, MTBEs, and TCEs, so that the new owners are not held liable later for damages and/or removal.

Finally, by becoming aware of recent changes, licensees should be aware that attitudes are changing about brownfields. Properties that might have been unmarketable just a few years ago may have substantial value today.

Where Can I Get More Information?

- The **EPA's Superfund Web site:**
  http://www.epa.gov/superfund
- The **CDC's Agency for Toxic Substance Disease Registry (ATSDR)** Web site is an excellent source about toxic substances, including links to the CERCLA registry of toxic substances: *http://www.atsdr.cdc.gov/*
- To locate **Superfund sites** in any region:
  http://www.epa.gov/superfund/sites/locate/index.htm
- The **EPA brownfields** Web site:
  http://www.epa.gov/brownfields
- The **Underwriters Laboratories** have tested products for more than a century: *http://www.ul.com/*
- The **Air Conditioning and Refrigeration Institute** develops and publishes technical standards for industry products: *http://www.ari.org/*

case study

Karen Alger's former residential client, Ervin Chambers, moved to another part of the state several years ago. Yesterday Karen received a call from Ervin asking for advice. It seems Ervin has decided to test the market for commercial building development.

Ervin has found a property that is attractively priced and is currently vacant. In fact, there aren't even very many weeds growing on the property. While walking the property, owners of nearby businesses came out to talk with him. It seems that the property used to house a poorly maintained car repair shop. Before that, one of them remembered, the railroad repaired electric transformers there. These folks think that the property might be a brownfield.

Ervin has never heard of a brownfield, although based on the color of the site, this seems to be one. However, the price is right, and the opportunity is there. How should Karen Alger advise Ervin?

1. What are brownfields?
    a. Economically depressed rural areas contaminated from pesticides
    b. Wetlands contaminated from a hazardous material
    c. Hazardous waste landfills designed for disposal of faulty USTs
    d. Economically depressed urban areas suffering from real or perceived contamination from a hazardous material

2. Karen should advise Ervin to
    a. make a very low offer with no contingencies.
    b. buy an option on the property for six months.
    c. make an offer contingent on documentation that he would have no future liability for cleanup.
    d. hire a consultant to verify the rumors before making any offer.

Student Comments

Please provide your comments regarding the basic principle(s) addressed in this case study, and its relevance to the subject matter generally:

_____

_____

_____

_____

Chapter 10 Review Questions

1. Which of the following is the oldest environmental law and is also called the Superfund Act?
   a. CERCLA
   b. SARA
   c. TSCA
   d. Brownfields Law

2. What is the purpose of the Hazard Ranking System (HRS)?
   a. Requires that any property placed on the list be scheduled for cleanup
   b. Determines the order in which sites will be cleaned up
   c. Assigns a numeric value to toxic waste sites to determine the likelihood a site may harm people or the environment
   d. Assures funding for cleaning up hazardous materials

3. Chlorofluorocarbons harm the atmosphere when they are released from
   a. air conditioners and refrigerators.
   b. air fresheners and household cleaners.
   c. underground storage tanks.
   d. car emissions.

4. Methyl tertiary butyl ether (MTBE) is added to gasoline to
   a. neutralize the lead fumes.
   b. improve combustion.
   c. extend engine life.
   d. increase miles per gallon (mpg).

5. What is a possible alternative for the use of methyl tertiary butyl ether (MTBE)?
   a. Ethanol made from corn
   b. Adding lead to the gasoline
   c. Poly-chlorinated-biphenyls (PCBs)
   d. Chlorine-containing CFC vapors

6. Brownfields are stigmatized properties because
   a. they are contaminated with a substance on the TSCA list.
   b. a felony, such as a murder, was committed on the property.
   c. they are perceived as possibly contaminated.
   d. they are located in the least desirable section of the urban area.

7. Under the Brownfields Law, new owners of a brownfield
   a. may utilize containment solutions instead of permanent remedies.
   b. are required to find a permanent solution for the toxic waste.
   c. are relieved of any responsibility for leaks or spreading contamination.
   d. may assign responsibility to a third party.

8. The presence of a TSCA listed product on real property
   a. enhances the value of that property.
   b. can negatively impact the value of the property.
   c. impacts the value of the property only if it is located inside city limits.
   d. is of concern only in rural transfers.

9. Recent brownfields legislations has the effect of
   a. rendering such properties unsaleable.
   b. enhancing the value of such properties.
   c. nothing on such properties.
   d. moving such properties into the residential market.

10. Under the Toxic Substance Control Act (TSCA), the EPA
    a. is required to test any new consumer products.
    b. can assign numeric values for hazardous wastes.
    c. can ban or restrict the manufacture and import of substances that pose an unreasonable risk.
    d. may impose a use tax on common toxic products to assist with their cleanup.

chapter eleven

Construction Issues

learning objectives

Upon completing this chapter, you will be able to

- explain the advantages and disadvantages of using EIFS.
- define an EIFS problem and list methods for correction.
- discuss problems with pressure-treated wood.
- list alternatives to using pressure-treated wood.

Key Terms

alkaline copper quat (ACQ)
arsenic
barrier EIFS
chromated copper arsenate (CCA)
chromium
drainable EIFS
exterior insulation and finish systems (EIFS)
pressure-treated lumber

What Is an EIFS?

Exterior insulation and finish systems (EIFS), often called synthetic stucco, are multilayered exterior siding systems used on commercial buildings and homes. EIFS have been used in Europe since the late 1950s and were only introduced into the U.S. market during the 1970s. Used almost exclusively in commercial buildings, by 2003, EIFS accounted for nearly 30 percent of the commercial exterior wall market in the United States. However, during the past 15 years, EIFS has increasingly been used in residential construction.

EIFS was successfully marketed on the basis of improved energy efficiency and flexible design possibilities. All EIFS use multilayered assemblies that incorporate insulation board and water-resistant sealers as part of their construction. Some EIFS reduce air infiltration by as much as 55 percent when compared to standard brick or wood construction. Unlike traditional stucco materials, EIFS come in virtually limitless colors and can be fashioned into complex shapes and designs. A skilled installer can create cornices, arches, columns, keystones, and similar accents that would be extraordinarily expensive with traditional stucco.

What Is the Problem with EIFS?

Few problems were reported when the first commercial EIFS were attached to masonry (concrete, cinderblock) or metallic framing components. Builders began to use EIFS in home construction, and they attached the EIFS to gypsum board (drywall), plywood, and oriented strand board (OSB), commonly called waferboard. Barrier EIFS, directly applied to the board using construction adhesives, were designed to seal the building from water penetration.

Unfortunately, water that penetrated EIFS became trapped behind it, causing many instances of mold buildup and water damage to the wood or gypsum board foundation. In 1995, numerous water intrusion problems were found in homes throughout the Southeast. As the number and age of homes clad with EIFS grew, the incidence of water-related problems mushroomed. This led to many large, successful lawsuits against EIFS installers and manufacturers.

What Causes the Water Penetration?

The most common source of water intrusion is around windows. Water enters either through the joint around the window where the EIFS materials butt the window, or via seams and joints in the window's construction. Other entry points include doors, gable vents, and other penetrations through the EIFS.

What is not clear is the reason for the problem. The EIFS Industry Member Association (EIMA) alleged that water penetration problems were due to incorrect installation, lack of training, shortcuts, or failure to follow manufacturer instructions. However, the National Association of Home Builders (NAHB) now states that homes with barrier EIFS can develop moisture intrusion problems even when constructed according to industry-recommended standards.

All sources agree that EIFS installation is definitely **not** a do-it-yourself project. They should be installed only by experienced applicators, those who have completed an EIFS manufacturer's training program certified by the Association of the Wall and Ceiling Industries (AWCI).

Are New EIFS Installations Still a Problem?

Figure 11.1 | EIFS Layers

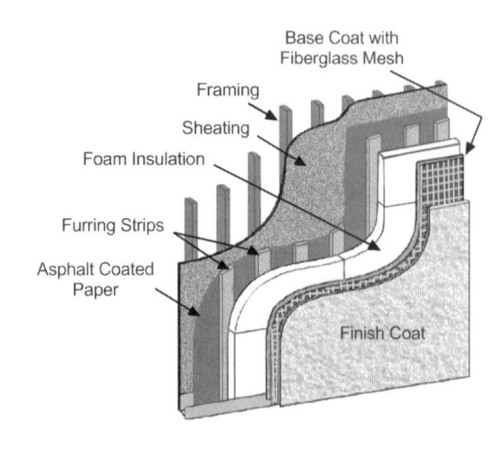

Some states and municipalities believe so and have placed restrictions on using EIFS in home construction. However, the industry is switching to a new method called drainable EIFS, which are designed to provide a way for water to escape IF it penetrates behind the EIFS. Drainable EIFS should dramatically reduce the occurrences of water buildup and subsequent damage.

The new method requires the following steps (see Figure 11.1):

1. Install starter track with drainage holes at bottom.
2. Apply asphalt-coated building paper.
3. Attach ⅛" x 3" plastic furring strips nailed through the foundation material (plywood, OSB, etc.) and into the framing studs.

4. Mechanically attach approved insulation foam board, minimum 1½" thick.
5. Apply durable synthetic base coat reinforced with fiberglass mesh.
6. Apply synthetic stucco-like finish coat.

■ How Can Owners Determine If Their Home Has EIFS Water Intrusion Problems?

Unless there are substantial, obvious signs, homeowners are unlikely to detect water penetration problems until they become severe. Detection must be done by professionals using two types of moisture meters: (1) a noninvasive device that scans through walls without penetrating the EIFS siding, and (2) a probe-type meter to accurately measure areas where the scanner indicates the presence of moisture.

Both the EIFS industry and the National Association of Home Builders recommend annual inspections to detect intrusions in their early stages should they occur. Be sure to use EIFS inspectors certified by the Exterior Design Institute (EDI) and the EIFS Industry Members Association (EIMA).

■ Can Leaking EIFS Be Repaired?

If there is substantial water intrusion and damage, the most cost-effective remedy may be to replace the EIFS with either a new drainable system or other siding material. If the problems are not severe, repairs should be made to prevent water intrusions in areas where testing shows elevated moisture readings.

If structural damage is involved, the affected materials should be replaced and the moisture dried before sealing any areas of water intrusion. Leak repairs usually involve the installation of flashings and caulking around doors and windows, chimneys, vents, areas where the roof and wall intersect, and other penetrations of the EIFS cladding.

■ What Is the Impact on Real Estate?

So far, few actions have been taken against real estate brokers or sales agents. However, homes clad with EIFS are aging which 1) increases the potential for developing leaks, and 2) their age may exceed the period under which they are covered by builders' warranties. A homeowner may then seek restitution from parties involved with the sale, and may be successful if adequate EIFS disclosures were not made. In other situations, the homes may be resold, thus presenting new opportunities to seek compensation from the sellers, real estate licensees, and home inspectors.

In a recent NAR *REALTOR® Magazine Online* article by Gary W. Jackson, "Your Best Defense? Prevention," Mr. Jackson suggests the following steps to avoid litigation:

■ **Ask Questions**—When dealing with a stuccoed property ask if it is traditional masonry stucco or EIFS. Ask if it has been tested or had any repairs made. If so, ask more questions.

■ **Make No Representations of Condition**—Making statements like "the house is dry" or "repairs have been made" can return to haunt you.

- **Encourage Buyers to Obtain an EIFS Inspection**—Suggest to the buyers that they may want to have the EIFS inspected, then suggest where they might find an inspector or more information about EIFS.

Where Can I Get More Information?

- **The Association of Wall and Ceiling Industries** Web site includes a roster of certified EIFS Mechanics (Installers) and the EIFS Inspectors. It also provides information on the availability of EIFS certification programs. *http://www.awci.org/eifs.htm*
- For legal information on issues concerning EIFS or attorneys in your region, check out the **EIFS Legal Network** Web site: *http://www.stuccolaw.com*
- The **EIFS Alliance** Web site offers a wide range of industry-related topics: *http://www.eifsalliance.com/*

What Is Pressure-Treated Lumber?

Pressure-treated lumber is the very familiar, green-tinged lumber used in millions of decks (see Figure 11.2), playsets, fences, picnic tables, and similar outdoor items. The greenish color associated with the lumber is a preservative called chromated copper arsenate (CCA) that is infused into the wood under high pressure. This protects the lumber from insects, bacteria, fungus, and water damage, thus making is suitable for outdoor use without additional protection. Approximately 90 percent of all treated lumber used in the United States is treated with CCA.

What Are the Problems with Treated Lumber?

Consumers are most concerned about the metal salts of chromium, copper, and arsenic that are used in making CCA-treated lumber.

Chromium and arsenic are both on the EPA Toxic Substance List and are known carcinogens. In fact, of the 275 substances listed on the CERCLA Toxic Substance Priority List, arsenic is ranked #1 and chromium #17.

Figure 11.2 | Deck Make with Pressure-Treated Wood

The arsenic in CCA-treated wood has been linked to bladder, liver, and lung cancer. A draft study by the EPA estimates that the lifetime risk of arsenic-related cancer in children who frequently crawl on structures made from CCA-treated lumber could be as much as ten times higher than the agency's recommended threshold for a "significant public health threat."

The potential exists for environmental and watershed contamination caused by the water runoff from CCA-treated structures. Some studies indicate that arsenic and copper concentrations in the soil close to CCA-treated structures are high enough to kill shrubbery and other vegetation. At this time the EPA verdict on CCA-treated wood is still pending, i.e., the EPA has "not concluded that CCA-treated wood poses an unreasonable risk to the public or environment."

■ What Is Being Done to Reduce the Risk of CCA-Related Health or Environmental Problems?

In February 2002, the EPA announced a voluntary decision by the lumber industry to phase out the production of CCA-treated lumber by December 31, 2003. As of January 1, 2004, the agency banned the use of CCA-treated wood for any residential purpose to facilitate the transition to alternative wood preservers. Many states and municipalities have replaced CCA-treated picnic tables and playground equipment at public parks.

■ What Are the Alternatives to Chromated Copper Arsenate?

Several major treated lumber producers have switched to alkaline copper quat (ACQ) which contains neither chromium nor arsenic. A few want to use acid copper chromate (ACC) which they believe is a better preservative, but does contain chromium. The EPA has not yet granted a "registration" to use ACC as a lumber preservative.

All of the alternatives are more costly than treated lumber. One alternative to treated lumber is to use woods such as redwood and cedar that are naturally resistant to insects and water damage. Unfortunately, these woods are slower growing than pines and firs normally used for making treated lumber, and thus raise concerns about harvesting old-growth timber. Other alternatives are to use plastics or other synthetic wood-like materials.

■ What Should Homeowners Do to Minimize Health Risks?

The EPA does not recommend replacing CCA-treated decks, playsets. picnic tables, or other structures. They do suggest that concerned homeowners might apply oil-based penetrating stains or silicone sealers on a regular basis to minimize the amount of CCA that leaches from the wood, and encapsulate metal salts on the surface of the wood. They also offer the following tips for minimizing exposure to CCA:

- ■ Treated wood should never be burned in open fires, stoves, fireplaces, or residential furnaces.
- ■ Always wash hands thoroughly after contact with the wood, especially before eating.

- Food should not come in direct contact with the wood.
- Sawing releases CCA-laden dust, so always wear dust masks and gloves when working with CCA-treated wood.

What Is the Impact on Real Estate?

As of this date we are unaware of any litigation against real estate licensees pertaining to CCA-treated wood. There have been some successful suits by lumber industry employees exposed to high levels of CCA in the workplace.

Licensees might want to provide health and risk-reducing information about CCA to prospective buyers with small children considering the purchase of a home with treated lumber structures.

Where Can I Get More Information?

- The EPA "pesticides" Web site provides links to wood preservers (CCA) and other pesticides. *http://www.epa.gov/pesticides/*

case study

Byron Parenti has been contracted by a young couple with two children under seven who are looking to buy their first house. Since this is the first home purchase for this young couple, they are understandably nervous. They know that inspections are expensive, and they don't have much money.

They want to find a property that offers a large backyard with room for children's play equipment. Imagine their surprise when Byron calls them about a new listing that "includes several pieces of playground equipment and a large outside deck." Plus, "the stucco will never need painting."

But Byron is concerned. At a recent continuing education seminar, he learned that treated wood can be considered a health hazard. Plus, he thought, wasn't stucco that never needed painting a possible concern? He decided to let the couple see the property before he raised these concerns.

Naturally, the buyers fell in love with the house, and became even more ecstatic when they saw the backyard and all of the equipment. They decided to make an offer on the spot. How should Byron continue?

1. Should Byron raise the EIFS issue, and why or why not?
    a. No, they have limited funds and would save money from never having to paint the synthetic stucco.
    b. No; after all, if there was a problem, the seller would have mentioned it.
    c. Yes, only an expert can readily discover EIFS problems.
    d. Only if Byron is directly asked about EIFS.

2. What is the problem with playground equipment made with pressure-treated wood?
    a. Wood never wears out
    b. More flammable than other wood
    c. Disintegrates quickly
    d. May leach arsenic and other poisonous chemicals

Student Comments

Please provide your comments regarding the basic principle(s) addressed in this case study, and its relevance to the subject matter generally:

_____

_____

_____

_____

Chapter 11 Review Questions

1. Commercial EIFS had fewer reported problems than residential EIFS because
   a. it was generally attached to cinderblock.
   b. it was attached to drywall and oriented strand board (OSB).
   c. commercial installers were more careful.
   d. there were fewer installations.

2. What is the primary negative problem with EIFS?
   a. Never needs painting
   b. Permits too much air flow
   c. Fireproof
   d. Traps moisture

3. What is the industry's solution to EIFS?
   a. Legislate standards for EIFS
   b. Drainable EIFS
   c. Phase out EIFS usage
   d. Use less durable products

4. Most of the EIFS lawsuits have been filed against
   a. real estate licensees.
   b. real estate appraisers.
   c. home inspectors.
   d. manufacturers and installers.

5. Where do most of the moisture leaks occur with EIFS?
   a. Walls that have buckled with freezing expansion and contraction
   b. Around windows and doors
   c. Seepage from incorrectly installed basement foundations
   d. Open sump pumps

6. In areas where EIFS is a problem, the licensee can appropriately make the following statement:
   a. You may wish to consider hiring a certified EIFS specialist to determine if this home has a problem.
   b. I've got the same brand of stucco on my house, and I haven't had a problem.
   c. The house appears dry from the outside, and we don't see any stains inside, do we?
   d. We should ask the sellers if they have had any problems with stains, smells, or leaks.

7. Chromated copper arsenate (CCA) in wood is indicated by
   a. testing with magnets.
   b. the greenish color or the wood.
   c. testing a piece of wood in the laboratory if installed prior to 1978.
   d. the seller disclosure.

8. Which of the following is a viable neutralizer or alternate for CCA pressure-treated wood?
   a. Application of fungicide
   b. Application of CCA removal polish
   c. Removal of the wood
   d. Plastic products

9. Which of the following should NOT be constructed with CCA-pressure treated wood?
   a. Picnic tables
   b. Fence around a yard
   c. Foundation reinforcements
   d. Fire towers

10. What law regulates CCA-pressure-treated wood?
    a. Superfund
    b. Lead-based Hazard Reduction Act (LBHRA)
    c. Clean Water Act Section 404
    d. There is no law

chapter twelve

Wetlands, Watersheds, and Endangered Species

learning objectives

Upon completing this chapter, you will be able to

- describe the importance of wetlands.
- explain the differences between watersheds and wetlands.
- summarize the problems to property owners when their land is designated wetland.
- explain "taking."
- identify the agency that can help farmers determine wetlands in order to retain available farm program benefits.
- explain the role of the Army Corps of Engineers regarding wetlands.
- explain the role of the EPA regarding wetlands.
- discuss the expanded application of the Endangered Species Act and its impact on private ownership.

■ Key Terms

aquifer	groundwater	watershed
Clean Water Act	Safe Drinking Water Act	wellhead protection
Endangered Species Act	storm runoff	wetlands

■ What Are Wetlands?

The official definition of wetlands is "those areas that are inundated or saturated by surface water or groundwater at a frequency and duration sufficient to support, and that under normal circumstances do support, a prevalence of vegetation typically adapted for life in saturated soil conditions." Often referred to as

Figure 12.1 | Typical Wetland

marshes, swamps, sloughs, and bogs, they can be man-made or natural, water hazards on golf courses or natural ponds, prairie potholes, or wet meadows.

Because "wetlands" is not a scientific term, each government agency has evolved its own definition of what constitutes a wetland. They can even include land that is dry for all but seven days a year. Since the 1600s, more than half of U.S. wetlands have been converted to farmland, drained or filled for housing developments and industrial facilities, and used as dumps.

Why Do We Need Wetlands?

Years ago, swamps, marshes, and other water-filled depressions were considered a source of mosquitoes and sickness and were drained or filled. Today, we know better. As a part of natural floodplains, wetlands can prevent flooding, help control erosion, filter out pollutants, clean drinking water, and provide homes for an abundance of wildlife. Often overlooked are other benefits: recreational, artistic, archaeological, historical, and scientific.

Wetlands help maintain and improve our water quality. They are frequently located between uplands and open water, and they intercept run-off and surface water and remove or transform pollutants through physical, chemical, and biological processes. Wetlands remove or reduce the following pollutants:

- **Nitrogen and phosphates**—Scientists estimate that wetlands can remove up to 70 to 90 percent of nitrogen and almost half of phosphate concentrations.
- **Biological oxygen demand (BOD)**—Sewage effluence, surface runoff, and natural biotic processes can cause a high level of BOD which in turn kills aquatic life. Wetlands remove almost 100 percent of BOD through the decomposition of organic matter or oxidation of inorganics.
- **Suspended solids**—Since nothing moves quickly in wetlands, suspended particles sink to the bottom and are prevented from moving downstream. Wetland vegetation can trap nearly 90 percent of sediment from runoff. Another benefit comes from pollutants being absorbed by suspended particles, thus removing even more pollutants from the water.

- **Metals**—Downstream from urban areas, forested wetlands remove metals from water. Between 80 to 90 percent of lead is bound to soil and sediments through adsorption by eel grass, other wetland vegetation, and muck.
- **Pathogens**—Threats to human health, fecal coliform bacteria and protozoans, enter wetlands via municipal sewage, urban stormwater, leaking septic tanks, and agricultural runoff. Wetland vegetation traps these organisms and they die: from exposure to the sunlight, low pH of wetlands, as food for other protozoa, and from the toxins excreted by the roots of some of the wetland plants.

What Is the Problem?

In the past, farmers and developers were encouraged to dredge and fill in wetlands, resulting in the loss of more than 50 percent of the wetlands in the lower 48 states, approximately 75 percent of which are privately owned. Building a consensus on wetlands policy has been difficult as environmentalists find themselves in conflict with property owners who cannot develop the land as they had intended.

Property owners have turned to the courts for relief, referring to the "takings" clause of the Fifth Amendment to the Constitution of the United States of America: "nor shall private property be taken for public use without just compensation."

Originally, courts only recognized takings claims when the property was physically acquired, and government actions for the purpose of protecting public health and safety, including environmental considerations, were not generally considered a "taking." Now, though, courts are saying that perhaps governmental regulations affecting private property may also amount to a taking.

Recently, courts have examined the character of the government's action and its effects on a property's economic value (reasonable, investment-backed expectations of the property owner). The following Supreme Court decisions support property owners in this issue:

- *Dolan v. City of Tigard (1994):* When Mrs. Dolan applied for permission to expand her family business, the city required her to donate land adjacent to a floodplain to create a public greenway and bike path. The Supreme Court ruled that there did not appear to be a "reasonable relationship" between the creation of the greenway and bike path and the impact of Mrs. Dolan's expansion; there was a "taking."
- *Lucas v. South Carolina Coastal Council (1992):* The U.S. Supreme Court ruled that a state regulation that deprives a property owner of all economically beneficial use of that property can be considered a "taking," and the owner must be compensated.

Are There Laws to Protect Wetlands?

Yes, the Clean Water Act Section 404 program regulates discharge of dredged and fill material to waters of the United States, including wetlands. Also, under the Swampbuster provisions of the 1996 Food Security Act, farmers may be denied access to specified farm program benefits if they convert or modify wetlands for agricultural production.

What Federal Agencies Supervise Wetlands?

The Natural Resources Conservation Service (NRCS, formerly the Soil Conservation Service) identifies wetlands on agricultural lands, and farmers can rely on a single wetlands determination by the NRCS to satisfy both 404 and Swampbuster. Farmers should check with NRCS before clearing, draining, or manipulating any wet areas on their land to make sure that they do not lose any farm program benefits. There is an appeal process.

The Army Corps of Engineers and the EPA have the lead for wetlands determination on nonagricultural lands. The Corps and the EPA jointly administer Section 404, which requires a permit from the Corps to discharge dredged and fill material into wetlands. The regulations were developed jointly with the EPA. Failure to get a permit or failure to comply with a permit can result in civil and/or criminal enforcement.

The EPA and the Corps share Section 404 enforcement authority. The agencies exercise their wetlands enforcement authority carefully, preferring to resolve violations through voluntary compliance and administrative enforcement. They reserve their Section 404 criminal enforcement authority for the most flagrant and egregious violations, as the following illustrates:

- *United States v. Pozsgai:* A Bucks County, PA, developer, Mr. Pozsgai ignored repeated warnings to get a Section 404 permit after purchasing land at a reduced price because it contained wetlands requiring a Section 404 permit. Neighbors, whose properties often flooded as a result of his wetland filling, assisted the case by videotaping his actions. Mr. Pozsgai was sentenced to three years in prison, assessed a fine, and ordered to restore the site upon his release.
- *United States v. Ellen:* As consultant and project manager, Mr. Ellen was responsible for obtaining all applicable environmental permits. He ignored warnings from his own engineers and supervised extensive excavation and construction work destroying wetlands and tidal marshes near the Chesapeake Bay. He was sentenced to six months in jail and one year supervised release.

What Are Watersheds?

Watersheds are areas of land that drain water, sediment, and dissolved materials to receiving bodies of water connected to them, including subsurface water. Watersheds vary from the largest river basins to just acres or less in size. They affect everything from recreational use of rivers and streams, to flood control, to quality and quantity of drinking water sources.

Groundwater and surface water are often directly connected, with water flowing back and forth from one to the other over time. The quality of groundwater directly impacts on surface water and vice versa. Any pollutants in either eventually end up affecting the other.

What Are the Issues Affecting Watersheds?

Worldwide, all watersheds including undeveloped land, rural areas, suburbs, and urban regions, are under stress from human-related activities. Some experts predict that water-related issues will become an increasing cause of world strife during the next 30 years. One-third of the world's population already suffers from insufficient amounts of clean drinking water.

One of the biggest watershed problems in the United States and much of the industrialized world involves stormwater runoff. Roads, parking lots, buildings, and other nonporous surfaces prevent water from seeping slowly into the ground, cleansing itself as it works its way to subsurface aquifers (subsurface groundwater available for wells and springs).

Instead, stormwater runoff picks up debris, petroleum-based products from road surfaces, animal waste, chemicals, and other pollutants, then deposits them into rivers, streams, and lakes. Eventually, more water is directed into the oceans, where it becomes salinated, further intensifying the problems.

■ What Laws Cover Wetlands and Watersheds?

The EPA believes water quality and ecosystem problems are best handled at the watershed level rather than at the individual water body or discharger level. With a few exceptions, most legislation concerning wetlands and watersheds was enacted in the '70s. Some of the major laws covering these issues include:

Figure 12.2 | Municipal Well

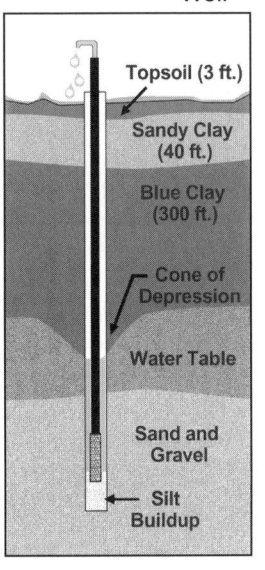

- Clean Water Act (1972)
- Coastal Management Act (1972)
- Endangered Species Act (1973)
- Safe Drinking Water Act (1974)
- North America Wetlands Conservation Act (1989)
- Agriculture Improvement and Reform Act (1996)

Municipalities are most concerned about protecting the underground aquifers and surface water bodies that are the sources of their drinking water. Accordingly, most states use provisions in the safe drinking water act to assist in source protection. The states can pass the funds provided by the law to localities for watershed and wellhead protection plans, provided they adopt policies and conform to guidelines set forth in the act.

Wellhead protection is a localized form of watershed protection. Localities are encouraged to adopt regulations and procedures to prevent pollutants from entering the underground aquifers that supply municipal wells (see Figure 12.2) drinking water. This is of particular concern in major farming areas where animal waste from lagoon spills and farm chemical seepage cause contamination that can rarely be corrected once the pollutants enter the aquifer.

■ What Is the Endangered Species Act?

Passed in 1973, the act was originally intended to protect endangered species on federal lands. Since then, the act has been used to control land use for the protection of hundreds, perhaps thousands, of certain species of fish and plant life. Habitats for any of these protected species may not be disturbed or modified. Although Congress stated that protected species were to be determined by "the best scientific and commercial data available," no standards were set, and the responsible agencies frequently made determinations without regard to economic consequences.

Another key provision allowed "any person" to bring a lawsuit to enforce the act. These "citizen suits" have been used to force government agencies to adopt new and stronger regulations. In the past, the courts only allowed lawsuits from those who wanted more, not less, protection for endangered species. A Supreme Court ruling in 1997 reverses this trend.

- *Bennett et al. v. Spear et al.:* Farmers were denied irrigation water during a drought in order to provide water in lakes and reservoirs to protect two species of fish. In the unanimous decision, the U.S. Supreme Court ruled that access to the courts is not just for "environmentalists alone" and while the law must protect endangered species, it must also "avoid needless economic dislocation produced by agency officials zealously but unintelligently pursuing their environmental objectives."

What Should a Property Owner Do?

Property owners most often affected by the Endangered Species Act are farmers and land developers. If the property is to be modified, the landowner should consult with the Fish and Wildlife Service. However, if federal money is involved, i.e., a loan underwritten by Fannie Mae, Freddie Mac, FHA, VA, SBA, FmHa, or any other federal agency, then the consultation is mandatory. There are serious consequences for failure to consult. For an unknowing violation, the fine is up to $500. Willful violations can result in fines ranging from $25,000 to $100,000 and possibly a year in jail. Informants can be paid, and anyone can sue the landowner for a violation.

How Does All of This Involve a Real Estate Licensee?

Anything that impacts on property ownership and use impacts real estate licensees. Developers have learned to their chagrin that they may not develop their plans, either because of clean water regulation or the Endangered Species Act.

Licensees working with commercial clients, farmers, and land developers should be aware of land use issues, for as noted in preceding cases, offenders risk fines, imprisonment, and costs to repair. It is useful for licensees to avoid making comments and decisions that are better left to regulatory agencies.

Where Can I Get More Information?

- The **EPA water-related home page** is: *http://www.epa.gov/owow/wetlands/*
- For breaking news and detailed, state-specific information visit the **Association of State Wetlands Management** Web site: *http://www.aswm.org/*
- Consult the **EPA Laws and Regulations** Web page for additional information on the federal laws affecting rivers, streams, and our water supplies: *http://www.epa.gov/win/law.html*
- The **Natural Resources Conservation Service** has a very-user friendly Web page geared to homeowners entitled "Backyard Conservation Tips." These can be obtained in printed form by calling (888) LANDCARE. *http://www.nrcs.usda.gov/feature/backyard*
- For information on wetlands in your area, consult the **EPA's Surf Your Watershed** Web page: *http://cfpub.epa.gov/surf/locate/map2.cfm*

- The **American Rivers** Web site offers a balanced and diverse range of topics on state, municipal, and federal water conservation efforts: *http://www.amrivers.org/riverconservation.html*

case study

Jason Wardell is a real estate agent who helped Hank and Jackie Lee move their in-house business from Milwaukee to a small town in Colorado. The home sits on a modestly sized lot on the north bank of a creek. The Lees enjoy fishing, so they built a shed on the bank. The creek is quite popular with outdoor sports enthusiasts.

The Lees, however, are not popular with the local community. They refuse to allow kayakers to cross their property to get to the creek. The Lees own about a dozen dogs of unusual breeds, some of which can be dangerous. The Lees also are active in a local group that meets regularly at their home to discuss ways to repeal government environmental regulations.

Recently the city council ordered the Lees to let the city build an access path on their property for kayakers. The Lees have refused, and have asked Jason to list their property for sale. Jason has told them that there are complications caused by the "takings" clause and regulations protecting wetlands and endangered species.

1. The purpose of the "takings" clause of the Fifth Amendment is to prevent the government from
   a. taking private property away from its owners.
   b. taking action against property owners who violate environment regulations.
   c. using private property for public purposes without just compensation.
   d. regulating the use of wetlands.

2. Property owners can be affected by regulations protecting wetlands and endangered species when they
   a. list their property for sale.
   b. house pets on their property.
   c. protest the severity of environmental regulations.
   d. modify their property without consulting appropriate federal agencies.

Student Comments

Please provide your comments regarding the basic principle(s) addressed in this case study, and its relevance to the subject matter generally:

_____
_____
_____
_____

Chapter 12 Review Questions

1. Wetlands can improve water quality by removing or reducing
   a. nitrogen and phosphates.
   b. asbestos.
   c. formaldehyde.
   d. radon.

2. Which law protects wetlands?
   a. Lead-Based Paint Hazard Reduction Act (LBPHRA)
   b. Clean Water Act Section 404
   c. Resource Conservation and Recovery Act (RCRA)
   d. Superfund Amendments and Reauthorization Act (SARA)

3. How can local authorities protect their drinking water?
   a. Drill deeper wells
   b. Create wetlands inside the city limits
   c. Wellhead protection
   d. Apply for Superfund monies

4. Rural cities are most concerned about pollution from
   a. factories.
   b. lead-based paint.
   c. nuclear waste.
   d. agricultural fertilizers and pesticides.

5. What contributes to water run-off?
   a. Parks and recreational areas
   b. Acres of cement-paved parking lots
   c. Low-impact buildings
   d. Demise of small towns

6. All of the following illustrate the value of preserving wetlands EXCEPT that they
   a. help control erosion and flooding.
   b. filter out pollutants.
   c. provide homes for wildlife.
   d. are sources of mosquitoes and sickness.

7. Which government agency is generally responsible for identifying wetlands on agricultural lands?
   a. Natural Resources Conservation Service (NRCS)
   b. Army Corps of Engineers
   c. Environmental Protection Agency (EPA)
   d. Fannie Mae

8. A developer can use a bulldozer to reshape the land if the developer
   a. provides a plan illustrating that the rearranged property will have at least 50 percent more value.
   b. has obtained permission from state and federal authorities.
   c. has properly filed the plat map with the recorder of deeds office.
   d. used the services of a certified environmental engineer to draw up the plans.

9. Which of the following pollutants often found in wetlands is a threat to human health?
   a. Pathogens
   b. Biological Oxygen Demand (BOD)
   c. Prairie potholes
   d. Wildlife

10. The most serious result of filling in a wetland without regulatory approval is
    a. possible imprisonment.
    b. conviction of a misdeamor.
    c. unfavorable publicity.
    d. minor fines.

chapter thirteen

Environmental Reports and Consultants

learning objectives

Upon completing this chapter, you will be able to

- explain the difference between an environmental impact statement and environmental site assessment.
- list several issues considered in an impact statement and its value to city planners.
- list at least three methods that site assessment professionals might use to discover possible contamination from previous usage.
- summarize the value of the site assessment to the seller, the buyer, and the lender.
- list three points to consider when hiring an environmental consultant.
- name at least five environmental engineer specialties recognized by the American Association of Environmental Engineers.

■ Key Terms

environmental engineer   environmental impact statement (EIS)   environmental site assessment (ESA)

■ What Is an Environmental Impact Statement (EIS)?

If a project is funded by federal money, the National Environmental Policy Act of 1969 requires a statement of the impact the project will have on the environment. Many state and local governments require similar statements for new projects or requests to change zoning.

An EIS can include comments about any or all of the following: noise, air quality, public health and safety, wildlife, and vegetation. Often included are analysis of anticipated changes in population density, vehicle traffic, energy consumption, the need for sewer and water facilities, employment, and school enrollment.

This information is useful to government agencies that may have to administer additional services, and has helped local municipalities appropriately charge impact and user fees to developers. If federal money is involved, there must be open hearings and the statements themselves must be available to the public.

Civic groups and the public have the opportunity to discuss the pros and cons of the proposed development. Having the information in advance allows for suggestions for modifications or alternatives.

■ What Is an Environmental Site Assessment (ESA)?

An environmental site assessment (ESA), or "due diligence" audit, is not at all like an environmental impact statement. Rather, it is an investigation done to determine if there are any environmental hazards or concerns that could affect the use of the property or impose future financial liability. Such preliminary research can protect the seller, the buyer, the agent, and the lender. If done prior to putting the property on the market, the seller can determine the cost of remedial work and factor that into sales negotiations.

Buyers want to limit exposure to unknown and expensive cleanup after purchase. Also, a thorough search is important to meet the "appropriate inquiry" element of the innocent landowner defense requirements of the Brownfield Act. In so doing, the buyer can limit liability for cleaning up a hazard left by a previous owner.

Lenders want to know the presence of any hazard or environmental consideration that might have a negative impact on market value. Therefore, it is imperative to use a certified environmental engineer to perform the assessment.

■ What Does an ESA Require?

The first step, a Phase I assessment, involves looking for potential contamination or noncompliance with environmental laws and regulations. If contamination is suspected or discovered, then a Phase II study should be conducted to include groundwater and soil analysis to ascertain the extent of environmental contamination. Finally, a third step, Phase III, involves site remediation. It is the most expensive study and often requires regulatory agency involvement and approval.

Since not all hazards are readily visible, and may have been covered over, a bit of sleuthing is required. For commercial and industrial properties, historical site usage is reviewed by looking at old aerial photographs, chain-of-title searches, topographic maps, and searching for old building plans, anything that might indicate a use other than that of the present time.

On-site inspections include looking around for brown and barren patches, odors, pipes protruding from the ground, or anything out of the ordinary. Regulatory agencies are consulted, and any personnel familiar with the site are interviewed. Neighboring and vicinity properties are scrutinized to determine if they could be draining pesticides or toxic wastes or harboring illegal dumping that could contaminate the subject property.

Both commercial and multifamily dwelling inspections include looking for asbestos, lead-based paint, and UFFI. The whole point is to discover any hazards that might be present on or impact the subject property.

■ Is There a Standard for Environmental Site Assessments?

Rule one is to hire a certified professional to conduct ESAs. As mentioned earlier, some proof of thoroughness is required to ensure that buyers and lenders meet the "appropriate inquiry" and "due diligence" criteria if legal action is ever taken. Additionally, if the buyers of a property have or hope to receive a brownfields site assessment grant, the study must meet the American Society for Testing and Materials (ASTM) Standard E1527-00, entitled "Standard Practice for Environmental Site Assessment: Phase I Site Assessment Process." The ASTM guideline mandates the following tasks:

- Site Reconnaissance
- Regulatory-Database Review
- Interviews with Knowledgeable Individuals
- Historical-Land-Title-Records Review
- Historical-Aerial-Photograph Review
- Topographic-Map Review
- Review of Regional and Local Geology
- Review of Regional and Local Soil Conditions
- Preparation of a Report Containing Findings and Opinion of Environmental Professional

■ What Are Some Considerations When Hiring an Inspector?

In the past, appraisers were expected (informally) to notice any environmental hazards that could adversely affect the market value of the property. Although appraisers may notice obvious problems, buyers and lenders are better protected by hiring specialists who are trained to find hazards such as UFFI, asbestos, proximity to industrial plants, sewer or water treatment plants, or commercial establishments using oil or chemical products.

The American Academy of Environmental Engineers recognizes (and offers certification courses for) the environmental specialists noted below. AAEE offers a free downloadable version of the *Environmental Engineering Selection Guide* that can be used to select environmental engineering experts. It identifies board-certified consulting firms and individuals available to the public for consulting assignments. The guide includes hyperlinks to firms or individuals with Web sites. This guide can be found here: *http://www.aaee.net/newlook/Electronic_edition_selec_guide.htm*

- AP   Air Pollution Control Engineer
- GE   General Environmental Engineer
- HW   Hazardous Waste Management Engineer
- IH   Industrial Hygiene Engineer
- RP   Radiation Protection Engineer
- SW   Solid Waste Management Engineer
- WW   Water Supply and Wastewater Engineer

As with hiring any contractors for work to be done, there are considerations and suggestions:

- Is the firm technically qualified? Does it meet its deadlines?
- Does the firm have staff with specific skills or experience required by the project?
- Ask to see reports previously done. Are they comprehensive? Do they identify the scope of assessment?
- Ask for references and talk to them. Were they pleased? Was the work done in a timely and cost-efficient fashion? Would they use the consultant again?
- Interview state and federal agencies, environmental attorneys, and colleagues in the given industry to help verify competency.
- Does the firm use subcontractors? Does this speed up the process?
- Is the consultant who will do the work an independent third party, separate from the company?
- Does the consultant have any certification?

■ When Do Licensees Get Involved?

The real estate licensee should encourage all parties to discover problems and defects as early as possible in the transaction to protect against any charges of nondisclosure. It is also useful for the licensee to encourage these investigations prior to entering into contracts. Quite apart from the pressure of meeting time requirements, there are more incentives for negotiation before a contract is signed.

Once a problem is discovered, many clients turn to their licensee for assistance in hiring a service provider. Licensees should investigate to determine if their state has certification requirements and, if so, to get lists of certified consultants.

As with any kind of recommendation for third-party services, real estate licensees should use caution and should limit themselves to furnishing a list and letting their clients make an informed choice about hiring. Also, whatever the task, they should encourage clients to specify a standard, probably that of the ASTM.

■ Where Can I Get More Information?

- The **Riley Guide at America's Career InfoNet** Web site has a very simple search system to provide state certification requirements for hundreds of occupations. When searching for inspectors or consultants it would be wise to check out this site to make sure the person you hire has the required certifications. *http://www.acinet.org/acinet/lois_start.asp*

case study

Samantha Oleson wants to purchase a parcel of land near the main highway just outside of a small town in Nevada. She is planning to build a small motel with recreational activities targeted to travelers with children. The parcel once was the site of a gas station and auto repair shop.

Samantha has asked a local real estate licensee, Clint Jones, if she needs to develop an environmental impact statement in order to purchase the land. If so, she wants Clint to serve as her agent. Clint said he would look into it. He told her she should begin conducting an environmental site assessment as soon as possible.

1. Samantha would benefit from a thorough environmental site assessment (ESA) primarily because it would enable her to
    a. determine the cost of remedial work and factor that into sales negotiations.
    b. discover any hazard that might have a negative impact on market value.
    c. avoid the liabilities and costs of an environmental due diligence audit.
    d. meet the "appropriate inquiry" element of the innocent landowner defense.

2. All of the following are normally parts of conducting an ESA EXCEPT
    a. looking for potential contamination.
    b. groundwater and soil analysis.
    c. developing an environmental impact statement.
    d. site remediation.

Student Comments

Please provide your comments regarding the basic principle(s) addressed in this case study, and its relevance to the subject matter generally:

_____

_____

_____

_____

Chapter 13 Review Questions

1. What is the purpose of an environmental impact statement (EIS)?
   a. Indicate the impact of the proposed project on the environment
   b. Discover any environmental concerns that could affect the use of the property
   c. Learn any possible future financial liability on the part of the developer
   d. Satisfy local zoning requirements

2. What is the purpose of an environmental site assessment (ESA)?
   a. Explain impact the project will have on the environment
   b. Discover any environmental hazards that could affect the use of the property
   c. Help local authorities determine appropriate impact and user fees
   d. Determine future growth patterns

3. With private money, a developer is planning to buy several parcels of land, and combine them to make one parcel on which he can build a mega super mall. Which of the following, if any, should he insist upon?
   a. Environmental impact statement (EIS)
   b. Environmental site assessment (ESA)
   c. Seller property disclosure statement (SPDS)
   d. Lead-based paint disclosures

4. A buyer wants to determine if there are any environmental issues, such as the presence of wetlands, prior to the purchase of a parcel of raw land. To ensure that he knows if any are present, the buyer should
   a. ask for a seller property disclosure.
   b. ask the county building inspector to inspect the property.
   c. hire a home inspector.
   d. hire a board-certified environmental engineer.

5. Which of the following offers certification for environmental specialists?
   a. American Academy of Environmental Engineers
   b. American Society for Testing and Materials (ASTM)
   c. National Association of REALTORS®
   d. Certified Commercial Investment Member (CCIM)

6. A consulting firm was asked to conduct a Phase I inspection. Which of the following will probably be studied?
   a. Need for sewer and water facilities
   b. Anticipated changes in population density
   c. Noise and air quality
   d. Brown and barren patches, odors, or anything out of the ordinary

7. A Phase II assessment would include
   a. a visual inspection of the property.
   b. groundwater and soil analysis.
   c. estimations of site remediation.
   d. searching the public documents for previous owners.

8. Interested community involvement is encouraged when conducting the
   a. environmental impact statement (EIS).
   b. environmental site assessment (ESA).
   c. seller property disclosure statement (SPDS).
   d. lead-based paint disclosures.

9. If asked for any kind of recommendation, how should the real estate licensee respond?
   a. Provide a list of qualified inspectors along with a ranking indicating the top rated on down
   b. Explain that most inspectors are not well qualified, and they can cause more trouble than they are worth
   c. Hand the buyer the telephone directory and say, "This not a decision that I can make for you"
   d. Limit themselves to simply providing a list and letting the clients make the decision

10. Why would an environmental engineer want to look at old aerial photographs?
    a. Learn historical use of the property and neighboring properties
    b. Population density
    c. Determine if asbestos is present on the property
    d. Discover any endangered species on the property

appendix A

Major Environmental Laws

More than a dozen major statutes or laws form the legal basis for the programs of the Environmental Protection Agency (EPA).

National Environmental Policy Act of 1969 (NEPA); 42 U.S.C. 4321-4347
NEPA is the basic national charter for protection of the environment. It establishes policy, sets goals, and provides means for carrying out the policy.

Chemical Safety Information, Site Security and Fuels Regulatory Relief Act;
Public Law 106-40, Jan. 6, 1999; 42 U.S.C. 7412(r)
Amendment to Section 112(r) of the Clean Air Act

The Clean Air Act (CAA); 42 U.S.C. s/s 7401 et seq. (1970)

The Clean Water Act (CWA); 33 U.S.C. s/s 1251 et seq. (1977)

Comprehensive Environmental Response, Compensation, and Liability Act (CERCLA or Superfund) 42 U.S.C. s/s 9601 et seq. (1980)

The Emergency Planning and Community Right-To-Know Act (EPCRA); 42 U.S.C. 11011 et seq. (1986)

The Endangered Species Act (ESA); 7 U.S.C. 136; 16 U.S.C. 460 et seq. (1973)

Federal Insecticide, Fungicide and Rodenticide Act (FIFRA); 7 U.S.C. s/s 135 et seq. (1972)

Federal Food, Drug, and Cosmetic Act (FFDCA) 21 U.S.C. 301 et seq.

Food Quality Protection Act (FQPA) Public Law 104-170, Aug. 3, 1996

The Freedom of Information Act (FOIA); U.S.C. s/s 552 (1966)

The Occupational Safety and Health Act (OSHA); 29 U.S.C. 651 et seq. (1970)

The Oil Pollution Act of 1990 (OPA); 33 U.S.C. 2702 to 2761

The Pollution Prevention Act (PPA); 42 U.S.C. 13101 and 13102, s/s et seq. (1990)

The Resource Conservation and Recovery Act (RCRA); 42 U.S.C. s/s 321 et seq. (1976)

The Safe Drinking Water Act (SDWA); 42 U.S.C. s/s 300f et seq. (1974)

The Superfund Amendments and Reauthorization Act (SARA); 42 U.S.C. 9601 et seq. (1986)

The Toxic Substances Control Act (TSCA); 15 U.S.C. s/s 2601 et seq. (1976)

answer key

Chapter 1 Case Study Answers

1. **A** Licensees, especially those representing buyers, should raise environmental concerns early in the transaction, thus permitting the client to research the issue before making informed decisions to test or not, to buy or not.

2. **B** Lead-based paint is of particular concern to buyers of childbearing age since children are most likely to be harmed by consuming lead excessively.

Student Comments:

Tandy is like the proverbial ostrich with its head in the sand, ignoring environmental issues. She should at least learn the basic issues in her area, Indiana. Then, she should discuss them with her client from another state asking if any are of particular concern to him. If Carl expresses any concern, Tandy should suggest that Carl start making plans to find reputable testers.

Chapter 1 Review Questions Answers

1. **A** The ideal time to raise environmental issues with the buyer is during the initial interview, prior to seeing any properties.

2. **C** Most states did not require disclosures in any real estate transaction until Congress passed the law requiring sellers to disclose any knowledge of lead-based paint and to provide a pamphlet to the buyers.

3. **D** Residential buyers are most likely to be concerned about lead-based paint issues, not wetlands, toxic waste sites, or underground storage tanks.

4. **B** In addition to expecting disclosure of structural defects, buyers now expect to be told of any environmental concerns regarding the property. They can pursue discovering county plans and what building permits might be required, but these are not issues about which the seller is realistically expected to provide information.

5. **D** Licensees should raise issues early in the process and suggest sources of additional information that assist the buyer in making an informed decision as to test or not.

6. **D** Licensees should help buyers realize that seller disclosure forms only ask the seller to disclose that of which the seller is aware. Buyers should determine which environmental issues are most important to them, and make decisions to test or not test based on that information.

7. **A** The real estate licensees should become aware of environmental laws and regulations and how to handle frequently encountered situations. Licensees get into trouble when they make decisions that are not theirs to make, such as advising not to test.

8. **D** The best place to start learning more about nearly every environmental hazard is the EPA's Web site or local office. Other agencies enhance the basic information, but the EPA is the place to start.

9. **B** Some states, particularly California, require that the licensee ask sellers additional questions under the presumption that licensees "should have

known" because there were certain red flags that would indicate a problem.

10. C The buyer is able to make better informed decisions with more disclosure, not less.

Chapter 2 Case Study Answers

1. D Only the Granatos family can make the decision to test or not test, since they are both paying for the test and will have to live with the consequences. The agent, Sandy, should not be drawn into making the decision, instead suggesting that the Granatos family consult with the local health department.

2. A Often the easiest way to eliminate a lead-based paint problem is simply to replace the contaminated doors, windows, moldings, baseboards, and so on.

Student Comments:

As soon as Sandy learned of the lead-based paint issue from the Granatos, she should have directed them to the local health department. If, after that, they were still very concerned, she might have made an effort to locate a property built after 1978, or helped them locate a professional tester.

Chapter 2 Review Questions Answers

1. A Lead always has the same qualities whatever day it is processed. The ideal time to raise environmental issues with the buyer is during the initial interview, prior to seeing any properties.

2. C Children under the age of six are most vulnerable to the effects of lead in the blood not only because their absorption rate is faster than that of adults, but also because their brains are in the formative state and are thus more vulnerable to toxic attack.

3. C Lead in the body is measured by a blood screen measurement and is expressed as micrograms per deciliter of blood (about ½ cup).

4. B The only way to quickly eliminate lead from the body is by chelation, a process whereby an ingested substance combines chemically with lead so that it can be excreted through the urinary system.

5. D The easiest method is to simply replace old doors, windows, trim, and other woodwork with new materials. The others are solutions, but they are expensive and require extra diligence.

6. D The lead-based paint disclosures are not required for housing built after 1978 and those units that have no bedrooms since it is unlikely that children will live in these units.

7. A Real estate licensees should become aware of environmental laws and regulations and how to handle frequently encountered situations. Licensees get into trouble when they make decisions that are not theirs to make, such as advising to test or not to test.

8. D The penalties are severe, up to $11,000 per incorrect signature or initials and/or imprisonment.

9. B The seller should answer honestly: I have no knowledge. The house may or may not contain lead-based paint and the only way to be sure it to have the house tested. This remains the concern of the buyer, however, who is encouraged to hire a tester to satisfy the buyer's concerns.

10. C The owner of any rental property built before 1978, regardless of how few rental properties are owned, is required to provide the disclosure. The landlords of apartments built after 1978, renovators of office buildings, and the seller of a house built after 1978 are exempt from the requirements.

Chapter 3 Case Study Answers

1. A The only sure way to know if there is radon in the home is to test for radon. Buyers should not rely on seller disclosures.
2. C The EPA's radon exposure "action level" is the level of radon exposure at which the EPA recommends mitigation. No one has to test, no one has to mitigate.

Student Comments:

The Wells naturally turn to their agent, Sol, to help them make sense out of the seller disclosure form. Sol should explain that "unknown" means that the seller has not tested for radon. His response was inappropriate. He should have said, "Radon can be an issue here as the presence varies from house to house. Here is a booklet to read and numbers that you can call for more information."

Chapter 3 Review Questions Answers

1. D Radon is a naturally occurring, odorless, colorless, radioactive gas, produced by the decay of uranium and radium.
2. C Neither the EPA nor current scientific consensus have been able to establish a "threshold" safe level of radon exposure, so the EPA recommends testing and mitigation if the readings are four or higher.
3. D The EPA has developed a shortened procedure using a 48-hour continuous device. Research indicates that about 94 percent of the time, the 48-hour test satisfactorily predicts whether a home's annual average is at or above 4 pCi/L.
4. B Radon is estimated to be present at levels higher than 4 pCi/L. in one out of 15 homes throughout the United States.
5. C The first step for radon mitigation is to seal cracks in the basement floors and foundation walls, before installing a PVC pipe into the ground.
6. A The best time to install abatement devices is during the construction of a new home. It is easier and less expensive to "hide" the PVC pipes during construction rather than retrofitting later.
7. D Real estate licensees should recognize that to test or not test is not a decision for the licensee to make. Concerned buyers can consult with local health officials. An installed system is a benefit, not a liability, since it is already in place should radon be detected.
8. A The best time to bring up any environmental concern, including radon, is during the initial interview with the buyer, before showing any properties. Buyers can indicate whether or not they will be testing and if they will be interested in mitigation.
9. D The EPA recommends that the radon testing device be placed in the lowest living level of the home. The basement would not be the best place IF laundry were done there only a couple of times a week.
10. C To keep everyone honest, an independent tester, not the mitigation contractor, should make follow-up radon testing 24 hours after the repairs have been made. The home inspector may or may not be the appropriate tester.

Chapter 4 Case Study Answers

1. **C** Only the buyer is responsible for discovery. If the sellers are not sensitive, they may not know they have a mold problem. Licensees are not responsible for determining mold contamination.
2. **D** The buyer should hire an inspector to look for issues that affect the buyer. The seller's property disclosure statement often lacks information important to the buyer, since the seller may genuinely not know about a problem that becomes important to the buyer.

Student Comments:

Sarah acted responsibly by noting the buyers' concerns, effectively communicating those concerns to prospective sellers, and insisting that the buyers follow through. While relatively rare, this true case study illustrates that buyers should take seriously their responsibility to discover any problems, especially with regard to mold. Sellers cannot disclose that of which they are not aware!

Chapter 4 Review Questions Answers

1. **A** Mold requires moisture, oxygen, warm temperatures, and a food source. It does not grow in sunlight.
2. **B** Today, buildings are constructed to prevent the loss of warm air in the winter and cool air in the summer. There is little airflow to help dry moisture and buildings become "petri dishes."
3. **D** Molds thrive on cellulosic food sources, such as carpet backing, wallpaper, particle board, and so on. They do not easily grow on glass or ceramic tiles of any kind. On the other hand, some molds do grow on the grout used between the ceramic tiles.
4. **B** Molds are a plant type of fungi, similar to lichens and mushrooms. They are biological pollutants.
5. **C** Asthmatic individuals who are allergic to mold spores may find that their asthma is greatly aggravated. Generally, mold sensitivity does not lead to cancer (radon and asbestos), impair neurological development (lead poisoning), or cause osteoporosis.
6. **D** The primary method used to control mold is controlling the moisture to below 55 percent relative humidity and increasing the airflow in the building.
7. **B** Ultraviolet rays in contained chambers can effectively kill mold spores. A HEPA filter merely filters out spores and the air exchangers do just that, exchange air, but neither they nor air fresheners actually kill the mold.
8. **A** For molds that can be cultured, air is drawn across a plate coated with agar (a growing medium) for a specific amount of time. The spores are then incubated for several days and the colony-forming units (CFUs) are counted.
9. **D** Only professionals properly trained should attempt to remove any mold contamination. Nonprofessionals could very easily cause the mold to spread throughout the building/home.
10. **A** There are no standards, and it is unlikely that the EPA or the CDC will be able to determine "acceptable" levels, inasmuch as there are so many types of mold, and individuals respond so differently.

Chapter 5 Case Study Answers

1. **D** Generally, professionals recommend that if the asbestos-containing material is in good shape and unlikely to be disturbed, the best course of action is to do nothing.
2. **C** Friable asbestos can be easily crumbled by hand pressure while asbestos is not easily released from nonfriable asbestos products.

Student Comments:

The seller was wise to have someone test for asbestos, and the seller is appropriately disclosing what he knows. However, he should not be offering advice to the buyers, who know a little but not enough. Fortunately, the buyers are represented by a real estate agent who should refer the buyers to a local health official, who, no doubt, will explain that leaving nonfriable ACMs in place is probably the recommended course of action. However, the buyers should be responsible for deciding the solution: to ask the seller to remove the asbestos, to remove it themselves, or to leave it in place.

Chapter 5 Review Questions Answers

1. **A** Asbestos is a naturally occurring mineral fiber whose Greek name means *inextinguishable*.
2. **D** Smokers exposed to asbestos are 50 times more likely to develop lung cancer than nonsmokers.
3. **B** Crumbled asbestos particles are so tiny that once airborne, they are very difficult to remove from the environment. Asbestos does not emit a gas, and exposure to water becomes an issue only if the water allows the material to become friable (easily crumbled).
4. **B** There is no law requiring testing for asbestos. Only professionals who are well trained should do the testing.
5. **A** The asbestos-related diseases are rarely curable. Unfortunately, the latency period is quite long, anywhere from 10 to 40 years.
6. **C** Unfortunately, products containing alternatives to asbestos such as fiberglass and mineral wool seem to cause the same kind of lung scarring and cancers that asbestos does. People should limit their exposure to these products as well.
7. **D** Any real estate licensee, commercial or residential, should have a working knowledge about asbestos. However, the licensee should be cautious about offering opinions regarding the presence of asbestos and whether or not to test or mitigate.
8. **B** If the asbestos-containing material (ACM) is in good shape and not likely to be disturbed, nothing should be done. The final decision should be made by a professional.
9. **C** By general definition, friable ACM (asbestos-containing material) contains more than one percent asbestos and can be easily crumbled by hand pressure. It is considered more dangerous because the particles can be loosened and broken down and become airborne.
10. **A** The federal law requires that any asbestos removal done in schools must be performed by certified professionals. There is no federal law that mandates residential testing or removal.

Chapter 6 Case Study Answers

1. **C** Given the situation, it is probably easier to avoid new construction since so many of the building products use formaldehyde in the manufacturing process. They can easily test for lead, and even if it is present, can take steps to keep it from chipping off and becoming a danger to them and their one-year-old.

2. **B** The agent should give the buyers a list of questions to ask a pest control company such as using natural and/or petrochemical-free insecticides or alternative treatments. A second course of action is to ask the sellers to verify that they have not used pesticides in the house, but they really cannot rely on the statement since the sellers may not remember and also cannot verify previous owner usage.

Student Comments:

First, Nancy should treat the buyers' concerns as material to the transaction. Nancy should already have a library of environmental information that she can use when buyers come in with specific issues. At the very least, she can refer the buyers to the local health department. The buyers should remember that formaldehyde eventually dissipates so Lily should be aware of any itching skin or breathing difficulties when viewing an older home.

Of the two concerns, lead-based paint versus volatile organic compounds, the easier to test for is the lead-based paint. So, Nancy can focus on showing older homes and having the buyers look for chipping and peeling paint that can be easily tested. It is entirely possible that the older home would not have any lead-based paint, and hopefully, will be free of formaldehyde as well.

Chapter 6 Review Questions Answers

1. **A** Formaldehyde-based resins are components of finishes, plywood, paneling, fiberboard, and particle board as well as floor coverings. Formaldehyde is found just about everywhere in the modern world. Excellent ventilation should assist in dissipating formaldehyde.

2. **C** Most striking about formaldehyde is its strong, pronounced odor. It quickly evaporates and is usually a problem shortly after the product enhanced by the formaldehyde is installed. Some estimate that 10 to 20 percent of the population is allergic to or sensitive to formaldehyde.

3. **D** The U.S. EPA has not set any safe or allowable standards at this time, although some Western European countries have set standards.

4. **B** Older products, such as the oak floors, are less likely to contain formaldehyde. However, the modern building materials were most likely manufactured using formaldehyde to add strength and fire retardance.

5. **D** Installation of new carpeting, draperies, or furniture should be done in the spring and summer so that windows can be left open as much as possible when the formaldehyde fumes are the greatest. Ventilation is the easiest and least expensive solution.

6. **B** The "–cide" in any word means to kill. Although some pesticides are restricted to use only by certified trained specialists, others are freely available even in grocery stores. Even the inert, i.e., inactive ingredients may be possible human carcinogens.

7. A Misapplication of lawn care products is the second largest cause of groundwater pollution, just slightly less than that caused by commercial farm herbicide use.

8. D Swallowing a pesticide usually causes the most serious problem.

9. B The Federal Insecticide, Fungicide, and Rodentcide Act (FIFRA) governs the registration of pesticides and prohibits the use of any pesticide product in a manner that is inconsistent with the product label. It does not mandate testing or determine any acceptable standards.

10. C Indoor air quality monitoring indicates that a complex mix of pollutants such as formaldehyde and carbon monoxide contribute to lower indoor air quality.

Chapter 7 Case Study Answers

1. A The licensee should suggest that the buyers have the well tested before they buy the property.

2. D There are no clear guidelines regarding disclosure of the potential problems of the adjacent gas station. However, since the possible contamination could affect the health and safety of the new owners and their children, many consultants recommend full disclosure.

Student Comments:

In many cases, the licensee on duty will be representing the seller since this is an in-house listing. The seller has indicated that the house has never been connected to the city water and sewer. Unsafe drinking water is a serious concern, so in order to avoid unpleasant recriminations later, the real estate company should recommend that the seller provide reports of the well water testing and also encourage any buyers to obtain a test prior to the purchase of the property.

The abandoned gas station next door to the property poses another problem. Quite possibly, many buyers would not realize, as these buyers do not, that gasoline could be leaking into the water supply. The listing agent, in order to protect the sellers from future liabilities, should recommend that the sellers make full disclosure of the adjacent abandoned property. If the sellers do not want to do this, the listing company should consider withdrawing from the listing.

Chapter 7 Review Questions Answers

1. C Humans can live less than a week without water, but nearly a month without food.

2. B Since rain cleans the air, the moisture is already compromised by the time that it reaches the ground. So, even rainwater is not pure. If the air was contaminated, then the rain probably was.

3. B Some of the most common water contaminants are manure and fertilizers containing high levels of phosphorus and nitrogen.

4. A Well water testing should be conducted in the spring after the snow has melted and during and after a rainy spell.

5. D Cryptosporidium and giardia are parasites that may be found in up to 97 percent of the surface water supplies. After ingestion, the cysts cause cholera-like illness with symptoms of diarrhea, headache, abdominal cramps, low-grade fevers, and more.

6. A The best solution for maintaining pure water is source protection, followed by filtration and chlorination and regular testing. Once chlorine was thought to be harmless, but we know today that it may combine with organic compounds forming by-products that may be harmful to humans.
7. D Watershed refers to the water drainage area.
8. D Bottled water is not required to meet federal standards and very few, if any, state or local standards. In fact, sometimes, it is municipal water in another form.
9. D There is no law requiring that well water be tested, but testing should be done on well water, and possibly even municipal water supplies.
10. A The Safe Drinking Water Act made it easier for the water treatment systems to comply with federal regulations. Annual reports must address violations of national primary drinking water regulations with respect to Maximum Contaminant Levels (MCLs), treatment techniques, significant monitoring requirements, and variances and exemptions.

Chapter 8 Case Study Answers

1. B The real estate licensee should have explained to the buyers that the seller's property disclosure is neither a warranty nor a guarantee. He should have advised them to obtain their own home inspection.
2. D The routine use of space heaters in the upstairs bedrooms should have alerted the licensee and the buyers to potential furnace problems or blockage in the ductwork.

Student Comments:

The real estate licensee made several errors. The first was "trying to sell the house" by relying on the sellers' disclosures. The licensee should have emphasized to the buyers that the seller's property disclosure is neither a warranty nor a guarantee, and that the important information is often missing. The second was in assuming responsibility for the home inspection and for confirming the sellers' declarations. Buyers should always be encouraged to hire their own home inspectors. Terry should be very thankful that nothing worse happened to the Tamoris.

Chapter 8 Review Questions Answers

1. D Combustion pollutants are primarily gases or particles that come from burning materials and include carbon monoxide, nitrogen dioxide, sulfur dioxide, and ash particulates.
2. C Symptoms of possible carbon monoxide exposure range from headaches, breathing problems, and increased risk of respiratory infections to death.
3. C Owners should schedule furnace inspections before the heating season begins, usually in the fall.
4. B While owners should follow the recommendations of the manufacturer, in general, the flues and chimneys should be inspected and cleaned at least once a year.
5. A If the entire fuel source is electricity, then no materials are being burned, hence little or no likelihood of producing combustion pollutants. However, gas, woodburning stoves, and kerosene space heaters are all possible sources of carbon monoxide.

6. A The carbon monoxide detector should be placed near the appliance that could produce carbon monoxide; in this situation, near the kitchen gas cook stove. Electric appliances do not produce combustion pollutants such as carbon monoxide.

7. A The first thing to do is to get people out of the environment into fresh air. Call health authorities and start CPR. Ultimately, the pollution source should be identified and repaired.

8. C If the carbon monoxide (CO) levels are high enough, the CO can replace the oxygen in the blood, causing death in a short period of time.

9. C Actually, air fresheners may do exactly the opposite of improving indoor air quality by contributing more pollutants. In order to improve air quality, owners should seek to control the source, improve ventilation, and install air cleaners.

10. D Methamphetamines are manufactured by easily obtainable materials such as antifreeze, and the labs are characterized by a sweet or ammonia-like smell. Coffee filters should normally be stained brown, not red. Red-stained coffee filters or linens were probably used to filter red phosphorus.

Chapter 9 Case Study Answers

1. B Neither the real estate licensee nor the buyers were skilled at recognizing the reason for the absence of grass. The inspection was worthwhile in pointing out a possible environmental issue. They wouldn't have known to raise the issue in their offer.

2. A Heating oil tanks are and were used by homeowners who used petroleum products to fuel their heating furnaces. Commercial concerns and industry also used stored petroleum products underground, but they were usually NOT heating oils.

Student Comments:

Kumar Joshi acted in a very responsible manner, first by insisting that his buyers hire a home inspector, and secondly, by encouraging them to follow up with specialized testing. The DEQ determines the responsible party for cleanup based on when the pollution is discovered. IF it is reported before closing, then the seller is responsible for the cleanup even if title passes before the pollution is cleaned up. However, if it is discovered after closing, then the buyer is responsible for the cleanup even if the buyer never used the tanks. Many states do offer financial assistance in order to ensure that as many tanks as possible are removed and the sites cleaned up.

Chapter 9 Review Questions Answers

1. D It is possible that a tank becomes "underground" due to wind erosion blowing in dust and debris, or the tank could have been partially buried originally.

2. A Although residential tanks are exempt from federal legislation, they can still leak and contaminate groundwater.

3. B Prior to the mid-1980s, most USTs were made of bare steel, which is likely to corrode, permitting the stored petroleum or hazardous materials to seep into the soil.

4. A Soil borings tests are most often recommended by environmental professionals for a real estate transaction. They produce the most accurate results.
5. B The LUST trust is funded by a 0.1 cent tax on each gallon of motor fuel sold in the country. By April 1995, about $1.44 billion had been collected.
6. C States have access to LUST trust fund money when they enter into a cooperative agreement with the EPA for administration, oversight of state programs, and cleanups.
7. B The BIG date was December 1998, when all tanks, even those installed prior to 1988, had to have spill, overflow, and corrosion protection.
8. D The United States Geological Society estimates that 96 percent of all UST sites contain some form of petroleum product. The American Petroleum Institute estimates that more than ten million homes with underground storage tanks store more than eight billion gallons of home heating fuel. They estimate that there are more than 200,000 (not two million) abandoned gas stations throughout the United States.
9. B Newly installed USTs must include safety features such as double wall construction of either corrosion-resistant metal or noncorroding synthetic materials like fiberglass or composites. The tank must be installed with overflow and spill prevention systems, as well as leak detection monitors.
10. A The presence of USTs must be disclosed to prospective purchasers and lenders, inasmuch as the presence or absence of USTs greatly affects the value and marketability of commercial and industrial sites. Disclosure includes tanks currently in use as well as abandoned ones.

Chapter 10 Case Study Answers

1. D Brownfields are economically depressed urban areas suffering from real or perceived contamination from a hazardous material.
2. C Ervin should make his offer contingent on gaining appropriate reports from competent professionals that would limit his future liability.

Student Comments:

Karen can explain to Ervin that brownfields are vacant urban areas that may have been contaminated with toxic products. Based on the casual conversation with surrounding owners, this may certainly be the case. Karen can explain that in the past, most buyers would have avoided even thinking about purchasing the property because the potential cleanup could be so expensive. However, the law recently changed, and this could present Ervin with a great opportunity.

However, Karen should recommend that Ervin find an agent who is more familiar with the area and to also hire an environmental consultant to ascertain what, if any, chemicals are still on the property. Most probably, Ervin can make an offer subject to a "due diligence discovery" time frame.

Chapter 10 Review Questions Answers

1. A The Comprehensive Environmental Response, Compensation, and Liability Act, passed in 1980, is commonly referred to as the Superfund Act. CERCLA created a tax collected from petroleum companies and this tax has been used to assist in cleaning up toxic sites.

2. C Based on initial waste site surveys, a number is assigned to determine the likelihood a site may harm people or the environment. HRS does not determine the order in which the sites will be cleaned or assure any funding for such an endeavor.

3. A Chlorofluorocarbons are used in air conditioners and refrigerators. Unfortunately, when they are released into the atmosphere, they ultimately deplete the earth's protective ozone layer.

4. B Methyl tertiary butyl ether (MTBE) is added to gasoline in order to improve combustion, thereby reducing air pollution.

5. A A viable alternative to MTBEs is ethanol, a product made from corn.

6. C Brownfields are areas near hazardous waste sites that are economically depressed from real or perceived contamination caused by the waste site.

7. A The Brownfields Law allows prospective purchasers and their lenders relief from liability for past contamination that they did not cause. They can consider containment remedies that could cost less than permanent ones.

8. B Many buyers and lenders avoid properties contaminated with TSCA-listed products since the potential cleanup can be so expensive. Fewer interested buyers usually means a lower price in order to make the property attractive.

9. B Recent brownfields legislation has changed attitudes about such properties, and some that might have been unmarketable a few years ago may have substantial value today.

10. C The EPA can ban or restrict the manufacture and import of substances that pose an unreasonable risk. It also may track the usage of such products.

Chapter 11 Case Study Answers

1. C Byron should definitely suggest to the buyers that they may want to have the EIFS inspected, then suggest where they might find an inspector or get more information about EIFS.

2. D Playground equipment made with pressure-treated wood may contain CCA that can leach arsenic, which has been linked to bladder, liver, and lung cancer, and arsenic-related cancer.

Student Comments:

Byron should have brought up environmental concerns at their very first interview. At that time, he could have discussed issues such as the EIFS concerns in his area, and should have ascertained if they would be hiring an inspector. Also, he needs to let the couple know at least what he learned at the seminar about pressure-treated wood since the children will be playing on the equipment. He should definitely encourage hiring a professional to determine if the structure behind the EIFS is sound. The couple may still decide to buy the property and that is fine, so long as they have learned as much as they can prior to purchase.

Chapter 11 Review Questions Answers

1. A Commercial EIFS was generally attached to masonry (concrete, cinderblock) or metallic framing components. Problems developed when builders began to use EIFS in home construction, attaching the EIFS to gypsum board (drywall), plywood, and oriented strand board (OSB), commonly called waferboard, which could harbor mold if damp.

2. D Once moisture gets trapped behind the EIFS, it has no way to evaporate, and eventually, the structure is weakened and deteriorates. The fact that it never needs painting and traps air are wonderful attributes.

3. B Industry is switching to a new method called drainable EIFS, designed to provide a way for water to escape IF it penetrates behind the EIFS. The occurrences of water buildup and subsequent damage should be greatly reduced.

4. D When the incidence of water-related problems mushroomed, many large, successful lawsuits were filed against EIFS installers and manufacturers.

5. B The most common source of water intrusion is around windows. Water enters either through the joint around the window where the EIFS materials butt the window, or via seams and joints in the window's construction.

6. A One specialist recommends that the buyers ask questions, and the licensee should make NO representation of condition and should strongly encourage the buyers to obtain an EIFS inspection.

7. B The greenish color associated with the lumber is a preservative called chromated copper arsenate (CCA) that is infused into the wood under high pressure. This protects the lumber from insects, bacteria, fungus, and water damage.

8. D The EPA does not recommend replacing CCA-treated decks, playsets, picnic tables, or other structures, but instead suggests that concerned homeowners might apply oil-based penetrating stains or silicone sealers on a regular basis to minimize the amount of CCA that leaches from the wood, and encapsulate metal salts on the surface of the wood.

9. A Consumers should avoid using food around CCA-pressure-treated wood. Although being phased out, it may not cause so much harm in fences, foundation reinforcements, or fire towers.

10. D There is no law. In February, 2002, the EPA announced a voluntary decision by the lumber industry to phase out the production of CCA-treated lumber by December 31, 2003. As of January 1, 2004, the agency banned the use of AAC-treated wood for any residential purpose to facilitate the transition to alternative wood preservers.

Chapter 12 Case Study Answers

1. A The purpose of the "takings" clause of the Fifth Amendment is to prevent the government from arbitrarily taking private property away from its owners.

2. D No one should add a building to property located near running water without first obtaining the necessary permits.

Student Comments:

Jason Wardell is correct in discussing the several issues confronting the Lees that can greatly impact the value of their property. The city council is now insisting that access to the river go across the Lees' property. Although they will still own the property, they will no longer enjoy complete privacy. They have built a shed near the creek, probably without a permit, and their dogs are going to be threatening to anyone looking at the property. This may be a tough sell.

Chapter 12 Review Questions Answers

1. A Wetlands intercept run-off and surface water and remove or transform pollutants through physical, chemical, and biological processes.
2. B The Clean Water Act Section 404 protects wetlands by regulating discharge of dredged and fill material to waters of the United States, including wetlands.
3. C Municipalities concerned with protecting the source of their drinking water use provisions in the Safe Drinking Water Act to assist in protecting the sources of their water, i.e., underground aquifers and surface water bodies.
4. D Overuse of fertilizers and pesticides is of particular concern in major farming areas where animal waste from lagoon spills and farm chemical seepage cause contamination that can rarely be corrected once the pollutants enter the water supply.
5. B Roads, parking lots, buildings, and other nonporous surfaces prevent water from seeping slowly into the ground, cleansing itself as it works its way to subsurface aquifers (subsurface groundwater available for wells and springs).
6. D Originally, people did fear the swamps as sources of mosquitoes and sickness, but not today. As a part of natural floodplains, wetlands can prevent flooding, help control erosion, filter out pollutants, clean drinking water, and provide homes for an abundance of wildlife.
7. A The Natural Resources Conservation Service (NRCS) generally identifies wetlands on agricultural lands, and farmers should check with NRCS before clearing, draining, or manipulating any wet areas on their land to ensure that they do not lose any farm program benefits.
8. B No one, farmers or developers, should rearrange the topography for any reason without first obtaining the permission of all relevant federal, state, and local authorities.
9. A Threats to human health, pathogens are fecal coliform bacteria and protozoans that enter wetlands via municipal sewage, urban stormwater, leaking septic tanks, and agricultural run-off.
10. A There are serious consequences for failure to consult. For an unknowing violation, the fine is up to $500. Willful violations can result in fines ranging from $25,000 to $100,000 and possibly a year in jail. Informants can be paid, and anyone can sue the landowner for a violation.

Chapter 13 Case Study Answers

1. D Only by insisting on an environmental site assessment (ESA) prior to purchasing the property can the buyers protect themselves from additional cleanup costs. She can also use the information to make an appropriate offer.
2. C Only federally funded projects are required to provide an environmental impact statement. An ESA normally involves looking for potential contamination, groundwater and soil analysis, and site remediation possibilities.

Student Comments:

Clint has offered good advice to Samantha. She can make her offer contingent on receiving additional information in the environmental site assessment (ESA) and can then determine IF she still wants to purchase the property. If she decides to proceed with the purchase, she can negotiate with the seller about any needed remediation.

Chapter 13 Review Questions Answers

1. **A** Any federally funded project must provide a statement of the impact the project will have on the environment.

2. **B** The ESA is the report from an investigation to determine if there are any environmental hazards or concerns that could affect the use of the property or impose future financial liability.

3. **B** The developer should insist on hiring a consultant to determine if there are any environmental hazards or concerns that could affect how he wants to use the property, and if there are any future financial environmental liabilities, i.e., environmental site assessment (ESA).

4. **D** This buyer should definitely consult with a board-certified environmental engineer to provide an ESA. Few states require sellers of raw land to provide any kind of disclosure, and any home or building inspector is not likely to have the skill to provide an ESA.

5. **A** The American Academy of Environmental Engineers recognizes (and offers certification courses for) the environmental specialists. The American Society for Testing and Materials (ASTM) has developed standards which must be met if the owner is seeking financial assistance to use a brownfield.

6. **D** A Phase I inspection seeks to discover any barren patches of land, odors, and anything out of the ordinary that could indicate a presence of an environmental hazard.

7. **B** After a visual site assessment, if contamination is suspected or discovered, then a second study should be conducted to include groundwater and soil analysis to ascertain the extent of environmental contamination.

8. **A** The environmental impact statement (EIS) should provide information to civic groups and the public, provide the opportunity to discuss the pros and cons of the proposed development, and allow people to make suggestions for modifications.

9. **D** Licensees should limit themselves to furnishing a list and letting the client make the decision.

10. **A** Historical aerial photographs are extremely useful when considering previous uses of the property. They would not be useful in determining population density, presence of asbestos, or the presence of any endangered species.

glossary

Abatement to make or become less in amount, intensity, degree, and so on.

Asbestos-containing materials (ACMs) materials containing asbestos that may be friable (easily crumbled) or nonfriable

Action level the air reading of radon at which the EPA suggests that a mitigation system be installed

Acronym (or initialism) a name made up of a series of initial letters or parts of words; for example, EPA (Environmental Protection Agency)

Aquifer an underground geological formation that contains a source of groundwater for wells and springs

Air exchanger a ventilation device that draws fresh air from the outside of a building and warms or cools the air using the stale air being exhausted to the exterior

Air sample testing a test for the presence of contaminants, such as mold and asbestos, that captures mold spores or asbestos fibers that can be quantified in the laboratory

Alkaline copper quat (ACQ) a preservative for treated lumber containing neither chromium nor arsenic

Arsenic a preservative used in treated lumber that is listed as number 1 on the CRCLA Toxic Substance List and is a known carcinogen

Asbestosis a disease evidenced by scarring of lung tissue by asbestos particles

Biological pollutants often invisible, living or were living, organisms that promote poor-quality indoor air, such as molds, dust mites, and other infectious agents

Brownfields economically depressed areas located near hazardous waste sites and may be stigmatized by a real or perceived contamination by the waste site

Brownfields Act federal law allowing certain contaminated industrial or commercial properties to become economically viable by allowing prospective purchasers and their lenders relief from liability for past contamination that they did not cause

Building-related illness (BRI) specific illnesses attributed to an identifiable material, product, or system in a home or building, such as Legionnaires' disease

Bulk sample testing a sample of suspected asbestos-containing material that is gathered by a certified inspector and sent to a qualified laboratory for identification

Carbon monoxide (CO) a colorless, odorless, poisonous gas produced by incomplete combustion

Carcinogen cancer-causing substance or agent

Centers for Disease Control (CDC) the primary federal agency charged with protecting the health and safety of people, providing credible information to enhance health decisions, and promoting health through other agencies

Cellulosic containing cellulose, the main constituent of plant cell walls, used in making paper, cardboard, and similar materials

Chemical spot test an inexpensive, destructive, and inexact method to test for the presence of lead-based paint by applying a solution to the painted surface and then observing the chemical reaction, if any

Chlorofluorocarbons (CFCs) used in air conditioners and refrigerators, responsible for depleting the earth's protective ozone layer; being phased out; leftover CFCs require proper disposal.

Chelation the process of ingesting a substance as a means of removing a heavy metal from the bloodstream; used in treating lead poisoning

Chlorine an inexpensive, easy-to-produce, corrosive, poisonous, greenish-yellow gas mixed into drinking water and swimming pools to destroy all animal and microbial life; not as harmless as once thought

Chromated copper arsenate (CCA) a greenish-colored additive that is infused into wood to protect the lumber from insects, bacteria, fungus, and water damage; may be linked to bladder, liver, and lung cancer

Chromium a substance used as a preservative in treated wood, listed as number 17 on the Toxic Substance Priority List, and a known carcinogen

Chrysotile a fibrous silicate mineral, a common source of asbestos

Clean Water Act 1972 federal legislation to first address pollution caused by stormwater run-off from the landscape

Coliform bacteria a group of bacteria primarily found in human and animal intestines and wastes, used as indicator organisms to show the presence of such wastes in water and the possible presence of pathogenic (disease-producing) bacteria

Comprehensive Environmental Response, Compensation, and Liability Act (CERCLA) federal law passed in 1980, creating the Superfund by imposing a tax on chemical and petroleum companies to fund hazardous waste cleanups

Combustion pollutants primarily gases or particles that come from burning materials and include carbon monoxide, nitrogen dioxide, sulfur dioxide, and ash particulates

Cryptosporidium a protozoan parasite that causes diarrhea

Decay life the period of time that it takes a radioactive substance to disintegrate or diminish its radioactivity

Deciliter one tenth of a liter, about 3½ fluid ounces

Dirty-socks syndrome Nonspecific growth of mold and bacteria on indoor coils and drain pans of heat pumps and air conditioners; name describes the smell

Disclosure forms forms mandated in some states requiring sellers to disclose certain known problems with the property

Drainable EIFS a system that allows water to escape if it penetrates behind EIFS; should reduce occurrences of water buildup and subsequent damage

Eletret electrically charged Teflon; serves as a source of high voltage in ion detection chambers

Encapsulation the use of sealers or coatings to enclose asbestos or similar materials to prevent exposure

Endangered Species Act 1973 federal law, amended in 1978 and 1982, to protect troubled species from extinction

Environmental engineer engineer trained to understand pollution control and the effects of humans and their activities on the environment

Environmental impact statement (EIA) a required study of the impact that any federally funded project will have on the environment

Environmental Protection Agency (EPA) the federal agency charged with protecting the environment

Environmental site assessment (ESA) an investigation done in phases to determine if there are environmental hazards or conditions that could affect the use of the property or impose future financial liability

Environmental tobacco smoke (ETS) smoke from tobacco that lingers in the air and as residue on carpets, woodwork, and walls, and produces a stain that is nearly impossible to remove

Epidemiology the branch of medical science concerned with the occurrence, transmission, and control of diseases

Exterior insulation and finish systems (EIFS) synthetic stucco used on commercial and residential buildings because of its energy efficiency and flexible design possibilities; water behind EIFS may permit mold to grow

Federal Insecticide, Fungicide, and Rodenticide Act (FIFRA) federal law that governs the registration of pesticides and prohibits the use of any pesticide product in a manner that is inconsistent with the product labeling

Fluoresce to emit light when bombarded with energy; in layman's terms, "glow in the dark" under ultraviolet light (black light)

Fluorspar a mineral sometimes fluorescent and often tinted by impurities; used in the manufacture of glass, enamel, and jewelry

Formaldehyde a colorless, organic chemical; indoor air pollutant with a strong pronounced odor; used in millions of products

Friable ACM material containing more than one percent asbestos; can be easily crumbled by hand pressure

Fungi organisms that recycle dead organic matter into useful nutrients; include mushrooms, rusts, smuts, puffballs, truffles, morels, molds, and yeasts

Giardia also known as giardiasis, an infection of the lower intestines caused by the amoebic cyst, which lives in water; symptoms include stomach cramps, diarrhea, bloating, loss of appetite, and vomiting

Groundwater subsurface water; any water stored in the ground below the water table

Half-life the average time it takes for one half of the particles in a sample of radioactive material to decay

Hazard rank system (HRS) a systematic method of evaluating waste sites for placement on the National Priorities List (NPL), determining the likelihood a site may harm people or the environment

HEPA filter high-efficiency particle acquisition filter that removes very small dust, mites, pollen particles, and more from the air

Hyphae the part of the fungus that feeds, grows, and replicates, consisting of cobwebby strands of white stuff

Infestation level the number of parasites living in or on a host

Ingest to take a substance or liquid into the stomach, i.e., to eat

Ionizing radiation radiation that produces charged particles (ions) in matter; materials that do this are radioactive

Ketone colorless liquid with an aromatic smell used as a solvent for lacquers, dyes, and adhesives

Lead-Based Paint Hazard Reduction Act (LBPHRA) federal law phased in by 1996 requiring that owners of properties built prior to 1978 notify occupants that lead-based paint may be a hazard in that property

Leach to remove or be removed from a substance by liquid

Lead blood levels lead measurements in the blood expressed as micrograms per deciliter

Lead poisoning illness caused by excessively ingesting lead either orally or through the skin

Liter a metric system unit of measure slightly smaller than one quart

LUST Trust trust fund created by Superfund Amendments and Reauthorization Act (SARA) to oversee cleanups by responsible parties and to pay for cleanups if the owner is unknown, unwilling, or unable to respond

Lymphosarcoma also called non-Hodgkin's sarcoma; a malignant tumor of the lymph glands

Mesothelioma rare cancer of the lining of the chest and abdominal cavity caused by asbestos

Methamphetamine a commonly abused, potent stimulant drug that is part of a larger family of amphetamines that exerts a stimulatory effect on the nervous system and can be used as a stimulant to the nervous system and as an appetite suppressant

Meth lab facility, such as a farmhouse, recreational vehicle, or the like, where methamphetamines are manufactured; can be as toxic as any EPA-registered hazardous waste site

Methyl tertiary butyl ether (MTBE) a gasoline additive to improve combustion, hopefully reducing air pollution from lead additives; highly soluble in water and can contaminate groundwater aquifers

Microbial VOC volatile organic compounds released by some molds

Microgram a very small unit of weight equaling one millionth of a gram; there are 454 grams in one pound

Mitigate to make less severe, to reduce a hazardous condition; used fairly interchangeably with abate or remediate

Mycotoxin toxic chemicals released by many fungi, especially molds; some are so dangerous they are used to make warfare nerve agents

National Priorities List (NPL) list and rankings of waste sites that may harm people or the environment

Nitrates chemicals that provide nitrogen for plants, much of which is lost to run-off and by leaching into the subsoil and into groundwater, and also can be a by-product of animal waste

Nonfriable ACM material containing asbestos that is tightly bound, such as asbestos vinyl floor tile

Pesticides chemicals used to kill pests; include plant growth regulators, insecticides, herbicides, fungicides, rodenticides, and disinfectants

Photosynthesis the process by which plants grow using sunlight absorbed by the plant's chlorophyll

Picocuries unit of measuring radioactivity

Polychlorinated biphenyls (PCBs) environmental contaminant; proven carcinogens used in many products including adhesives, paints, and fluorescent light fixtures; production halted in 1977

Pressure-treated lumber lumber infused with CCA to protect the wood from insects, bacteria, fungus, and water damage; can be used outdoors without additional protection

Radium a radioactive element found in pitchblende, carnotite, and other uranium ores, and is used in radiotherapy and in luminous paints; radium decays to radon

Radon a colorless radioactive element of the rare gas group, the most stable isotope of which, radon-222, is a decay product of radium; is used as an alpha particle source in radiotherapy

Safe Drinking Water Act (SDWA) federal law passed in 1974 to protect public health regarding the availability of safe drinking water

Sick building syndrome (SBS) symptoms that affect at least 20 percent of building occupants during the time they spend in the building and which go away when they leave the building and cannot be traced to specific pollutants or sources within the building

Smelting the process of extracting metal from ore by heating

Soil borings test samples of soil are removed from the site and sent to an EPA lab to determine the presence of petroleum; recommended in a real estate transaction

Stack effect natural upward movement of warm air in a building that acts as a vacuum drawing inside soil gas with radon

Storm run-off surface run-off of snow or rain that discharges untreated into our creeks, rivers, lakes, estuaries, bays, and oceans

Subslab suction active soil depressurization to remove radon gas before it seeps into the building

Soil vapor test air pulled through several small shallow holes drilled near an UST and analyzed to determine petroleum content

Spore a reproductive body, produced by bacteria and fungi, that develops into a new individual

Stachybotrys highly toxic slimy black mold; generally grows outdoors

Sump pump a pump placed in a catch basin to remove groundwater or flood water from basements

Superfund Amendments and Reauthorization Act (SARA) 1986 federal act renewing and amending CERCLA providing the EPA with new enforcement authorities and negotiating tools

Tank integrity test semiannual testing of gas station tanks to determine if any gasoline is leaking from the underground tanks; not recommended for a real estate transaction

Target housing housing built prior to 1978 that may contain lead-based paint; such disclosure must be made during a sale or rental

Toxic poisonous, harmful, or deadly

Toxicity a measure of the ability of a substance to induce injury to living tissue

Toxic Substances Control Act (TSCA) 1976 federal law giving the EPA authority to track industrial chemicals and permitting the EPA to ban or restrict the manufacture and import of toxic substances that pose an unreasonable risk to human health and the environment

Trichloroethylene (TCE) a nonflammable, colorless liquid with a sweet odor and taste used as a solvent for cleaning metal parts and in the dry-cleaning business, contaminating many underground water sources; likely to produce cancer in humans

Uranium a radioactive metallic element used chiefly as a source of nuclear energy by fission of the radioisotope {uranium-235}; uranium decays to radium

UST underground storage tanks, tanks with at least 10 percent below ground level, often containing petroleum products that may leak and contaminate the soil and water

UFFI urea formaldehyde foam insulation

Volatile organic compounds (VOCs) gases emitted at room temperature from certain solids or liquids containing a variety of chemicals that compromise indoor air quality

Watershed specific land areas that drain water, sediment, and dissolved materials to receiving bodies of water connected to them

Wellhead protection a strategy designed to protect public drinking water supplies by managing the land surface around a well where activities might affect the quality of the water

Wetlands areas of land that are sufficiently wet to support vegetation typically adapted for life in saturated soil conditions

X-ray fluorescence a reliable method of testing paint history on-site using an expensive x-ray instrument